Stanley Wood

An Unattended Journey, or Ten Thousand Miles by Rail

Stanley Wood

An Unattended Journey, or Ten Thousand Miles by Rail

ISBN/EAN: 9783744796101

Printed in Europe, USA, Canada, Australia, Japan

Cover: Foto ©Andreas Hilbeck / pixelio.de

More available books at **www.hansebooks.com**

AN UNATTENDED JOURNEY

OR

TEN THOUSAND MILES

BY RAIL

A TOUR BY FOUR YOUNG LADIES

FROM THE LAKES . ACROSS THE PRAIRIES . OVER THE ROCKIES . THROUGH
THE DESERTS . AMONG THE SIERRAS . TO THE PACIFIC COAST
A SOUVENIR OF TRANS-CONTINENTAL TRAVEL
RICHLY ILLUSTRATED

BY

CHICAGO
THE WHITE CITY ART COMPANY
1895

A LEGEND BY WAY OF PREFACE.

THERE is a Celtic legend which relates that in the golden age of chivalry a maiden, unattended and bearing a wand in her hand surmounted by a diamond of great price, walked unharmed through the length and breadth of Ireland. This legend is cherished by all loyal Celts as an illustration of the courage and purity of their women and of the honor and honesty of their men.

In these modern days it would be rash for us to boast that such an experience could find a duplicate, yet, in a sense, it is duplicated in a great many instances every week in every month of every year. The environment is of course different, but in this little story of a spring time journey, we may find set down the experiences of four young ladies who crossed the continent unattended by male escort and met on every hand most courteous treatment and most kindly counsel and found in all their travels no one to molest them or to make them afraid.

Such a journey as that, the incidents of which are here recorded, can be taken at any time by anybody and so thoroughly systematized are the methods of transportation and so perfect the arrangements for personal safety and comfort that a truthful relation of the experiences of any one tour may be taken as a faithful representation of what every one may expect to experience under like circumstances.

Faithfulness in the statement of facts is claimed for this narrative and the reader of this little book can rely on the accuracy of what is herein set down. The object of the writer has been to give the traveler, however learned in the literature of the road or, on the contrary, however inexperienced in the matter of journeying, such information as will prove of value and prepare the way for an intelligent and enjoyable trip across the continent.

The illustrations with which this work is embellished are all made expressly for this book, from photographs taken by special artists from the most striking of the objects of interest which abound to a most remarkable extent along the lines of travel herein described.

The reader is referred to the final pages of this book for special indexes and valuable tables of statistics.

The author wishes to give credit in this place to the photographic artists whose work is represented by the illustrations which add so much of value to this record of travel. The photographs were made by the artists whose names are appended: W. H. Jackson, C. R. Savage, Lock and Peterson, Hook Photo. Co., O. F. Tyler & Co., W. R. Cross and John A Lowel and Co.

Every tourist who makes the trip across the continent desires to secure souvenirs of the journey and knowing this fact the author has endeavored to make this volume such a record of facts and such a collection of beautiful, accurate, and attractive views that it will be recognized by all as a most appropriate and interesting souvenir of the transcontinental journey.

AN ELKHORN MONUMENT, ESTES PARK, COLORADO, 60 MILES FROM DENVER. BURLINGTON ROUTE

CHAPTER I.

HOW WE GOT TO DENVER.

"From land of lakes to land of gold,
From meadow lands to mountains old,
Toward the setting sun we fly,
My bonnie Jane and I."

—Old Song

"IT all came about naturally enough and yet it was not exactly the conventional thing to do." The speaker was a young society lady and she was relating to a friend the circumstances which led up to the taking of a pleasure trip of ten thousand miles, from Chicago to San Francisco and return, including side journeys to places of interest en route across the continent. The unconventional part of the journey lay in the fact that it was taken by four young ladies entirely without the attendance of gentlemen escort and because of this fact they had called it their "Unattended Journey."

"It was a trip for health and pleasure, and as my father was exasperatingly well and exasperatingly busy, he couldn't attend me, hence I must either go alone or not at all. In this emergency I opened correspondence with a friend and sent a letter something like the following:

CHICAGO, ILL.

Dear Joan:—I'm planning a trip to California. You in Denver are so near that haven of rest that you can go with me just as easy as not. The question is will you do it?

Your friend,

JUDITH.

"The answer came back to me in four days and was as follows:

Dear Judith:—Yours received. Will I take a trip to California with you? Won't I!

Your friend

JOAN.

P. S. I've asked dear Julia, she's living in St. Louis now, to join us. She'll do it sure. Can't you find a fourth, it's so much more cheerful to have a quartette, then we can take a section all to ourselves in the sleeper, and there won't be any horrid man to sit in the front seat with his back to the engine and stare us out of countenance; we can play whist without a dummy, we can order two portions of roast duck at a la carte dinners and have enough for four We can buy four apples for a dime and not become deadly enemies over the division of the fourth, as we'd be sure to do if there were three of us in the party. Take my word for it we'll have a much better time as a quartette. 'There's luck in odd numbers, says Rory O'More.'

Your chum,

JOAN.

"I saw the force of Joan's argument and after some diplomatic correspondence induced Jennie B., an old school friend of mine, residing in Omaha, to join our party. So it was settled that Joan, Julia, Judith and Jennie should make this "unattended journey."

"Quite a party of jays."

"Do you mean it? No. I remember you never use slang, so I'll forgive you. We arranged it so that we should make our rendezvous the Brown Palace Hotel in Denver, and from that center city of the mid continent continue our journey to the western rim washed by the waves of the Pacific Ocean.

"In solemn conclave one bright spring day we met at Denver in a private parlor of the Brown Palace Hotel, which by the way is well worthy of its name, for it is a palace of bronze, onyx, and dark pink sandstone, and there we formed a commune by the rules of which each member was bound to observe the requirements of liberty, equality and fraternity. Everything was to be held in common, no one was allowed under any pretext whatever to keep any information concealed upon her person, and if any one should by accident see anything the others hadn't seen, she must at the first opportunity tell the rest of us all about it. Thus it happened, that in order to start fair, I had to describe the journey from Chicago to Denver via the Burlington. Jennie related what she had observed in her trip from Omaha to Denver, over the Union Pacific, and Julia told the story of her experience en route from St. Louis to our place of meeting:

FALL RIVER, ESTES PARK, COLORADO. BURLINGTON ROUTE.

"Chicago to Denver! It's a long cry from the city on the lake to the city by the mountains, but actually, girls, it seemed more of a task to get from our house on Michigan Avenue to the Union depot in Chicago, than to make all the rest of the journey.

"I felt like the little girl in the story who said she rode a 'little way in the cars and all the rest of the way in the wagon.' I wanted papa to buy my ticket, check my baggage, order a carriage, and attend to all the preliminaries of starting, but he coolly informed me that, as this was to be an unattended journey, the sooner I began to look after my own affairs the sooner my own affairs would be looked after by me. I actually believe he thought I'd give up the journey concerning which he had never shown any marked degree of enthusiasm, but he was very much mistaken as I respectfully, but firmly informed him.

"'I'll find out all about it before night, papa,' said I. 'Thank goodness I've got a tongue.'"

Teton Range from the East. Burlington Route.

"Only one?" said he.

I declined to notice this remark and merely said, "This trip has been planned in a broad, general way and now I'm going to examine into the minute but necessary details."

> "If a woman will she will,
> You may depend on't,
> And if she won't she won't,
> Why that's the end on't."

chanted my unfeeling parent, as he lighted a cigar and started off down town for his office. It wasn't long before the dark villain pursued him and I found myself standing with palpitating heart in front of the Burlington ticket office, corner of Clark and Adams Streets. I *did* hate to make the plunge and walked on half a block to gather courage for the undertaking; feeling braver I walked back again and stood in front of the entrance only to find myself more reluctant than ever to open the door. Then, like the little girl who disliked a

AMONG THE FOOT-HILLS, ESTES PARK, COLORADO. BURLINGTON ROUTE.

ESTES CONE, ESTES PARK, COLORADO. BURLINGTON ROUTE.

cold bath, I said 'rats!' and scared myself in. A nice young gentleman came forward and asked what he could do for me.

"Is the President of the road in?" I asked as nonchalantly as I could.

"No, Miss, this is not the President's office, but if you wish to purchase tickets or make any inquiry as to rates or routes I shall be happy to assist you."

"That young man, girls, must have been a mind reader. How else could he discover that I didn't want to see the President. I knew at once that there wasn't any use in trying to deceive him so I told him all about the unattended journey, and the way he helped me out was just too lovely for anything.

"First he sold me a ticket with a great number of coupons to it, and every coupon stamped on the back with a cunning little red circle filled with big initial letters and some figures, and then he folded it up in a most miraculous manner so that it looked like an accordion in a state of collapse. As you know

Devil's Slide — Union Pacific System, near Ogden.

TUNNEL NO. 3, WEBER CAÑON, UTAH, ON UNION PACIFIC SYSTEM.

by experience with your own tickets, these folds were so artfully made that never by either the greatest care or merest accident could the uninitiated, after unfolding it once, ever fold it up in its original shape.

"This ticket was good for a length of time amply sufficient for an extended stay on the Pacific Coast, allowed stop over privileges, as the young man explained 'here, there and everywhere,' and imperatively demanded passage for the bearer on first-class trains.

"After accomplishing this, he sold me a Pullman ticket to Denver and arranged for a man to call at my home to get and check my baggage, which was the end of all worry about that. Then he engaged a carriage, which was to convey me later in the day down Michigan Avenue, across town and over the bridge to the Union depot.

"After dinner, that evening, papa looked across the table at me with a superior smile and said, 'Well, my dear, when do you depart on this unattended ridiculosity?'

"In about an hour" I replied, in my most businesslike traveling man tone. Girls, I just wish you could have seen his face when I said *that*. He insisted on going with me to the train, though I assured him it wasn't at all necessary, but all the same I was very glad to have him with me, and when he kissed me good by at the station with moistened eyes, there was a lump in my throat, and I too, I must confess, shed some unmanly tears. But *n'importe*, as we used to say in boarding school, when we knew French and everything else under the sun, much better than we'll ever know anything again. Off went the train and I felt that now, indeed, the unattended journey was begun.

"Pullman cars, like tall silk hats, have a strong family resemblance, and the sleeper to which I had been allotted was no exception to the rule. I never could tell papa's spring hat from his autumn head gear, when both were newly ironed, and I have never learned the marks of individuality

BLUFFS OF GREEN RIVER, UNION PACIFIC SYSTEM.

From the Union Depot up Seventeenth Street, Denver, Colo.
Population, 175,000. Altitude, 5,285 Feet.

which differentiate the Pullman, "Azimuth" from the Pullman "Zenith," or the "Baalbec" from the "Cavilero." And yet there are differences. Its the atmosphere literally and figuratively, a hot car, a cold car, a careless conductor, an indifferent porter, make all the difference in one's enjoyment of a journey. These elements of discomfort were absent in the through-to-Denver coach on the Burlington Flyer, and, with a clear conscience, a comfortable couch and a sense

CATHEDRAL SPIRES. GARDEN OF THE GODS, NEAR MANITOU, COLO.

of safety and protection I slept the sleep of the just, while the train thundered along at the rate of fifty miles an hour toward the Missouri river, on the western bank of which I was to meet my dear Jennie.

"What a lovely peroration," exclaimed Jennie.

"Don't interrupt the speaker," said Joan.

"Silence in the coaht," murmured Julia, in her soft southern voice, and with such a funny attempt at judicial

Gateway Garden of the Gods, D. & R. G. R. R., Looking West. Pike's Peak in the Distance.

BALANCED ROCK, GARDEN OF THE GODS, MANITOU, COLO.

sternness that we all laughed heartily, after which I took up the broken thread of my story.

"I was dreaming that I had found 'Aladdin's Lamp,' and had summoned the Genie, who appeared in the shape of a giant Nubian, with coal black skin and glowing eyes, and made me a most humble salaam, saying:

"What askest thou of thy slave and the slave of the lamp?"

"Sing me," said I, "the song that Israfael sings to the angels in Paradise."

"Then the Nubian opened his mouth and I heard an awful

THE GRAVE OF H. H. CHEYENNE MOUNTAIN, 7 MILES FROM COLORADO SPRINGS.

voice chanting 'La-a-st ca-ll for breakfast in the d-i-n-ing c-a-a-r a-h-e-a-d. L-a-s-t c-a-l-l for b-r-e-a-k f-a-s-t,' and I awoke and I knew it was a dream. I realized also that my breakfast would be nothing but a dream if I wasted any more time, and making a hasty toilet, I hurried into the dining car ahead. Oh, the comfort of a good warm breakfast in one of those first-class hotels on wheels, a well-conducted dining car! Glimpses of the flying landscape without; of the early birds who tried to catch the speeding train as if they were under the impression that it must be the succulent worm which the proverb promises to all early birds; of the bright spring sunshine gilding the earth with glory; of the sky, blue and cloudless and serene, and within; the sheen of polished silver, the shimmer of snowy linen, the delicate aroma of delicious coffee, the polite solicitude of ebony hued servants, the abundance of luscious fruits from all lands temperate and tropic,

Manitou Springs, Colo., 80 Miles from Denver, via Denver & Rio Grande R. R.   Elevation 6,321 feet

Cog Railroad up Pike's Peak, Manitou, Colo.

PIKE'S PEAK, COG WHEEL R. R. TIMBER LINE.

and the presence on demand of every luxury in the way of tempting and appetizing food.

"Hear, hear!" cried Jennie, "why don't you compose a poem about that breakfast?"

"She cahn't," said Julia.

"Perhaps *you* can," said I loftily.

"Of coahse I can," replied Julia, "and I will;

> Of all the things, I do decla'h,
> The finest thing I evah saw,
> Was breakfast in a dining cah.

Now! What do you think of that?"

"A great deal of truth but not a bit of poetry. Now don't interrupt me, that's a good girl, or I'll never get through my story.

"After breakfast I returned to my car, found that the porter had made up the section, dusted the seats, put all of my little belongings in neat and convenient shape and left an extra pillow ready for my use.

Mother Judy, Monument Park, 9 Miles from Colorado Springs, Colo.

SUMMIT OF PIKE'S PEAK, 88 MILES FROM DENVER. ELEVATION 14,714 FEET

"What can one do on the Burlington Flyer *en route* across the continent? Anything, everything, except to step off and take a walk. The views from the car window are ever changing, always entertaining. The scenery of Illinois and Iowa, through which States the line extends to the Missouri river, is interesting and suggests pleasant thoughts giving one a wide-horizoned idea of the beauty and productiveness of these two commonwealths. The broad well-tilled acres, the large comfortable farm houses, almost manorial in appearance, the green wheat fields, the waving corn, the woodlands casting grateful glooms of shade, the rolling hills growing bolder as the murky flood of the Missouri is approached, the wide prairies, giving glimpses through dotting, dimpling groves of the distant, dim horizon; all these one beholds for a moment, loses in a moment and finds again, repeated with endless variations the next moment. This fleeting panorama reminds me of the song about the bubbles:

Bubbles light, bubbles bright
　　See them come and go;
Airy, fairy dainty things
　　Floating to and fro;
Golden in the sunshine,
　　Silver in the shade,
Lovely, fair and debonaire,
　　Of such things dreams are made.
We touch them and they vanish,
　　Vanish like a dream,
Fair and frail and fleeting,
　　Shadows on a stream—

"There I've forgotten the rest of the verse, girls, but that's enough to give you the idea."

"But it's not enough and I insist on your remembering the rest," said Joan.

"Can't do it, its gone, gone like—"

"A bubble," murmured Julia.

Pike's Peak Avenue, Colorado Springs, Colo., on Denver & Rio Grande R. R. Antler's Hotel at Base of Pike's Peak.

High Bridge of the Loop above Georgetown, Colo., Union Pacific, Denver & Gulf R. R.

AMPHITHEATER, WILLIAMS CAÑON, MANITOU, COLO.

"I thank thee, Jew, for teaching me that word."

"My name is Julia," remarked that literal young lady, "and I'd thank you not to contract it to Ju," whereupon we all laughed and I was requested to "Mosey along" with my story.

"There are two things that impressed me strongly during my journey from Chicago to Omaha, and these were the vast resources of the farming country and the prosperous and attractive appearance of the towns and cities along the route. Such a journey is a liberal education to any one who has not already a competent knowledge of the richness and stability of this great nation. I have no doubt that there has been a reflex action in the building up of the country along the line of my touring. I mean by this that the railroad has assisted in the growth of the country and the richness of the country has assisted in the strengthening of the railroad. In any event the facts remain that there is no more prosperous country on the continent than that contained within the State

THE LOOP, UNION PACIFIC, DENVER & GULF R. R., NEAR SILVER PLUME, COLO.

UTE PASO, MANITOU, COLO. THE OLD INDIAN TRAIL TO THE SPRINGS.

GREEN LAKE, ABOVE GEORGETOWN, COLO., UNION PACIFIC, DENVER & GULF R. R., NEAR THE LOOP

The Snowy Range from the Arkansas Valley near Buena Vista. Denver, Leadville & Gunnison R. R.

RAILROAD CUT THROWN OUT WITH ONE BLAST, ON THE FLORENCE & CRIPPLE CREEK R. R.

ENTRANCE TO CRIPPLE CREEK CANON ON THE FLORENCE & CRIPPLE CREEK R. R.

lines of Illinois and Iowa, and there is no better equipped and no more thoroughly satisfactory and efficient railroad than the Burlington.

"These thoughts were superinduced by a pleased study of the landscape and the contemplation and discussion of a most excellent lunch in the dining car. Comfort of mind and body contribute to philosophical musings and I found myself pleased with my surroundings and at peace with all the world. When the evening shadows began to fall we crossed the Missouri river, broad and muddy and shallow, wandering carelessly along between widely separated bluffs with thousands of acres of cultivated bottom lands margining the stream but a few feet higher than the turbid flood. When the train rolled into the station at Omaha, there was Jennie on the platform waiting to greet me. You may be sure I was glad to see her, for say what you will, a journey all alone is a lonesome journey.

After talking eagerly together for a few minutes, Jennie said:

"Now I must go?"

"Go?"

"Yes, and get on board my train for Denver, I'll be there before you, for I'm going over the Union Pacific."

"You'll not beat me there," said I, "for I shall speak to our conductor and have him jog the engineer's elbow. Goodbye, you mean thing, I thought I'd have your company the rest of the way."

Jennie laughed and disappeared. Soon the train pulled out and we were off for the long night run through Nebraska. Before darkness settled down I got a good idea of the rich agricultural country through which we were passing. A good dinner and a sound night's sleep followed, and in the morning the porter told me we were in Colorado and would

SAIL SHIP ROCKS, PLATTE CAÑON, NEAR DENVER, ON THE DENVER, LEADVILLE & GUNNISON R. R.

GOLD MINER'S CABIN, CRIPPLE CREEK, COLO.

soon reach Denver. The mountains were in view like pale blue clouds, dashed with white, the snows of eternal winter banked against the western horizon. A leisurely toilet followed by a leisurely breakfast, filled in the time, and before the daylight was three hours old Denver was announced and the first long stage of my journey had been completed.

"There, girls, my story is done and it's Jennie's turn to take up the moving tale."

"Once upon a time," began Jennie, "there was a cruel Princess who delighted in torturing her subjects. She'd tell a story clear through to: 'and they were married and lived happily ever after' and then she would ask some one else to finish the story."

"What do you mean?" interrupted Judith.

"You know, well enough. You've told how you go to the cars, what you saw there and what you saw afterward. What have you left me to tell?"

ROTUNDA OF MINERAL PALACE, PUEBLO, COLO. THE PALACE WAS ERECTED AT A COST OF $250,000, AND CONTAINS A MAGNIFICENT MINERAL EXHIBIT.

"Old King Cole;" Statue made of Colorado Coal and Flint, the Mineral Palace, Pueblo, Colo.

"The truth, the whole truth and nothing but the truth concerning your journey from Omaha to Denver."

"That's all very well, but I think you spoke rather disrespectfully of the Missouri river, and you didn't say one word about the Mississippi, either."

"Well, we crossed that in the night at Burlington and I was sound asleep besides. Julia can tell us about that for I'm informed that it's quite an institution at St. Louis."

"Institution, indeed!" said Julia. "You'll speak disrespectfully of the zodiac, next."

"You're all out of order," said Joan severely, "Jennie has the floor."

"Yes, I'm floored, that certain."

"No levity, please, proceed with your narrative."

"From Omaha to Denver sweep the great plains in such majestic vastness that only the mysterious expanse of the ocean can be used as a comparison. Not many years ago these broad savannahs were the grazing grounds for the buffalo and the antelope, and the home of the not less wild and much more savage red men. My father has chased the former and been chased by the latter on more than one occasion. Even the span of my life, not a long one, reaches back to the time when western Nebraska was a land weeks' distant from the river, and to be visited by men with arms in their hands and stout hearts in their bodies. Now, *voila! Behold!* Palace sleepers, vestibuled coaches, fast through trains, dining cars! Piff! we leave Omaha, Paff! we're in Denver.

"Now, the farmer and the followers of pastoral pursuits have occupied the land, and savage nature is yielding on every hand to the prowess of the plow."

"Prowess of the plow is good," interrupted Judith sententiously.

"Yes, my dear, the great western kingdom of Nebraska has tried it and pronounced it good. As one rides hour after hour beholding waving fields of maize on either hand, extending in undulating billows of grateful green to the far horizon's rim, one realizes that here corn is king. Of this kingdom in

Trout Fishing, Wagon Wheel Gap, Colo.

Wagon Wheel Gap, Colo., on Denver & Rio Grande R. R. Elevation 8,440 feet. Distance from Denver, 311 miles. Health and Pleasure Resort. Hot Springs of Great Medicinal Qualities.

the west Omaha is the metropolis, Lincoln the capital, and the Union Pacific Railroad the *via maximus.*

"I never see the tassels of the corn nodding to the breeze like some ladies' favor on a Knightly crest, but there arises in my mind the figure of Mondamin, and I recall Longfellow's beautiful poem of the origin of maize. You remember, girls, that wonderful fast of Hiawatha's, and how on the fourth day of his fasting he lay in his lodge by the Big-Sea-Water, exhausted, and his mind filled with vague dreams and weird imaginings. Then he gathered his remaining strength together and gazed with undazzled eyes upon the splendors of the sunset.

> 'And he saw a youth approaching
> Dressed in garments green and yellow,
> Coming through the purple twilight,
> Through the splendor of the sunset;
> Plumes of green bent o'er his forehead,
> And his hair was soft and golden.
> Standing at the open doorway
> Long he looked at Hiawatha,
> Looked with pity and compassion
> On his wasted form and features,
> And in accents like the sighing
> Of the south wind in the treetops,
> Said he, "O, my Hiawatha!
> All your prayers are heard in heaven,
> For you pray not like the others;
> Not for greater skill in hunting,
> Not for greater craft in fishing,
> Not for triumph in the battle,
> Not renown among the warriors,
> But for profit of the people,
> For advantage of the nations.
> From the Master of Life descending,
> I, the friend of man, Mondamin,
> Come to warn you and instruct you
> How by struggle and by labor
> You shall gain what you have prayed for.
> Rise up from your bed of branches,
> Rise, O youth, and wrestle with me!'

"And so they wrestled in the twilight and Hiawatha felt

Toltec Gorge, Denver & Rio Grande R. R., near Alamosa, Colo. Train is shown entering Tunnel near Summit of Peak at Right. Height of Walls, 1,800 feet

new courage as he struggled with this strange foe and at length prevailed and overthrew him.

> "'Tis enough!' then said Mondamin,
> Smiling upon Hiawatha,
> 'But to-morrow when the sun sets,
> I will come again to try you!'

"On the morrow, and yet again on the next day, Mondamin came for the gladatorial trial with Hiawatha and was overcome on each occasion and after the third trial:

> 'Then he smiled and said: 'To-morrow
> Is the last day of your conflict,
> Is the last day of your fasting,
> You will conquer and o'ercome me;
> Make a bed for me to lie in,
> Where the rain may fall upon me,
> Where the sun may come and warm me;
> Strip these garments, green and yellow,
> Strip this nodding plumage from me,
> Lay me in the earth and make it
> Soft and loose and light above me.
> Let no hand disturb my slumber,
> Let no weed nor worm molest me,
> Let not Kahgahee, the raven,
> Come to haunt me and molest me,
> Only come yourself to watch me,
> Till I wake, and start, and quicken,
> Till I leap into the sunshine.'

"And on the seventh day of Hiawatha's fasting Mondamin came and the two wrestled for the last time together and

> 'Suddenly upon the greensward
> All alone stood Hiawatha,
> Panting with his wild exertion,
> Palpitating with the struggle;
> And before him, breathless, lifeless,
> Lay the youth with hair disheveled,
> Dead he lay there in the sunset.'

"The grave was made as was commanded and Hiawatha returned to his wigwam and broke his fast. But he did not forget the grave of Mondamin and day by day he went to watch and tend it. He kept the dark mould soft above it and drove away the predaceous crows and ravens.

Phantom Curve, Denver & Rio Grande Railroad, near Alamosa, Colo.

'Till at length a small green feather
From the earth shot slowly upward,
Then another and another,
And before the summer ended,
Stood the maize in all its beauty,
With its shining robes about it,
And its long soft yellow tresses,
And in rapture Hiawatha
Cried aloud, "It is Mondamin!"

CAÑON OF THE RIO LAS ANIMAS. D. & R. G. R. R. SILVERTON BRANCH
THE ANIMAS RIVER IS SHOWN FLOWING BETWEEN WALLS 1,500
FEET HIGH.

Yes, the friend of man, "Mondamin!"
Then he called to old Nokomis
And Iagoo, the great boaster,
Showed them where the maize was growing,
Told them of his wondrous vision,
Of his wrestle and his triumph,
Of his new gift to the nations,
Which should be their food forever,
And still later, when the Autumn

Changed the long, green leaves to yellow,
And the soft and juicy kernels
Grew like wampum hard and yellow,
Then the ripened ears he gathered,
Stripped the withered husks from off them
As he once had stripped the wrestler,
Gave the first Feast of Mondamin,
And make known unto the people
This new gift of the Great Spirit.'

NEEDLE MOUNTAINS FROM ANIMAS CANON.   DISTANCE FROM DENVER
483 MILES.

"I can't tell you about the manor houses that Judith describes so enthusiastically, because manor houses are the product of generations and of national prosperity, while this new west has not more than one generation to look back upon and its prosperity is too recent to manifest itself in such outward symbols. But I can tell you of the planting of roof trees that in the process of the suns shall shadow manor houses which shall shelter the descendants of the hardy pioneers. I can tell you of broad and fertile acres won by toil from savage Nature, of baronial holdings, that every year grow in comeliness and value, of the building of a new State, the dawning of a new star, the birth of a new empire.

"The journey from Omaha to Denver is an object lesson of more than common significance. It opens the mind of the observing traveler to facts and fancies new and vast and suggestive. It shows how this great Nation has grown great. It is the first chapter of a marvelous historical romance. And further than this it sheds a new and brilliant light on the old poet's query: "What constitutes a State?" Not moated walls, not iron gates, not pomp, not panoply, nor pageant, but *men*. Men with honest hearts, earnest souls, toiling hands, dauntless courage, who dare the dangers of the frontier, who endure the privations of new comers in a new land, and who, like the coral builders, give their lives as component parts of the magnificent structure which they help to rear.

"After we had gotten well into Nebraska and had whirled through a number of prosperous looking towns and villages, the darkening landscape reminded me that night was approaching and the hour of dinner near at hand. I can bear testimony to the truth of Judith's report as to the excellence of the *cuisine* on board the diners, for the dinner the Union Pacific cooks furnished was most excellent and the service of the best.

After a hearty meal, prolonged to an unconscionable length because of the unusual excellence of the viands prepared for my enjoyment and refreshment, I settled down in my section of the sleeper for a good night's rest and before long, was sleeping as soundly and as comfortably as if I was at home and not flying along on wings of steel and steam toward the Rocky Mountains and the land of gold and silver.

In the morning I awoke in Colorado, and looking out of the window saw such an expanse of brown, gravel sprinkled plains that I wondered how man or beast could find subsistence on that seemingly sterile waste. But I also saw herds of cattle busily engaged in browsing and their plump sides

Uneva Lake, Colo., on Denver, Leadville & Gunnison R. R.

MT. ABRAMS ON TOLL ROAD IRONTON TO OURAY.

OURAY, COLO., GOLD AND SILVER MINING TOWN. ELEVATION, 7,721 FEET. DISTANCE FROM DENVER, 380 MILES.

showed that they had found something to eat that made them fat and comfortable. That something I learned was buffalo grass, a curly dry forage that looked but little more nutritious than the gravel among which it grew. But buffalo grass is more nutritious than the best of timothy and as fat producing as grain. I learned another fact, and that was that this gravelly soil was as fertile as the famed valley of the Nile, when once it had been supplied with plenty of water by means of irrigating canals.

LAKE SAN CRISTOVAL, NEAR LAKE CITY, COLO.

As I was gazing out of the window a sedate looking young man shouted "Buffalo!" Of course everybody scrambled to see the novel sight, when he added, "are said to be extinct." This joke never fails to work, and I am betraying a confidence in telling you about it now.

After breakfast the sedate young man tried to create another riot by shouting "The Rocky Mountains!" but we were all too shrewd to be caught by his little game. Later

THE TREE IN THE ROCK, FLORENCE & CRIPPLE CREEK R. R.

"BIG BEND," ON THE OURAY AND SILVERTON TOLL ROAD. THIS WAGON ROAD WAS MADE THROUGH MOUNTAINS AT AN EXPENSE OF $10,000 A MILE, WHERE DIFFICULT ROCK WORK WAS DONE.

on we discovered that we in reality had been sold a second time, for the mountains actually were in sight and we had missed the opportunity of catching the first glimpse. Soon however we saw an undulating line of intenser blue drawn against the azure of the western sky and we knew that we beheld the great Snowy Range of the Rocky Mountains.

"My journey from Omaha to Denver was nearly an accomplished fact, and such had been the pleasure and comfort of the trip that I felt almost inclined to regret that the end was so near. Surely the railroads have reduced travel to its lowest terms of discomfort and rendered that which, in former days, was a subject of dread, a positive source of almost unalloyed enjoyment.

When the long vestibuled train of the Union Pacific stopped in the Denver Union Depot, the polite porter assisted me to disembark, and as I was crossing the platform I met Judith.

"When did you get here?" I exclaimed.

"A minute ago. When did you get here?"

"Two minutes ago! I told you I'd be here first."

"Nonsense!" said Judith, "you merely got me to commit myself first, that's all," and so the question as to which of us made the best time is still *res adjudicata*.

"Now, Julia, tell us about your journey from St. Louis," said Joan.

"Once upon a time—" began Julia, whereupon Judith interrupted.

"I rise to a point of order."

"State your point," said Joan.

"I object to the word time. The railroads have annihilated it."

"The objection is well taken," ruled Joan.

"Well, I'm not so sure of that," said Jennie. "I know they *make* time on the railroads, for I heard our conductor say the train was making good time, but I'll not dispute the point. Judith has said that I would tell you about the Mississippi river, but I shan't do anything of the kind. Every-

Sultan Mountains and Baker's Park, with Silverton in the Distance. Elevation, 9,224 feet. Distance from Denver, 405 miles. Population, 2,500.

body knows everything concerning the 'father of waters,' and the most striking thing about the river at St. Louis is the big bridge.

"I left home on the through Burlington train and there's one thing about my journey that overtops anything you girls have told, and that thing is, that I took the train from the very largest Union Depot in the whole world!"

"How about the St. Pancras station, London?"

"Its not in it, or rather it could be put in it and it

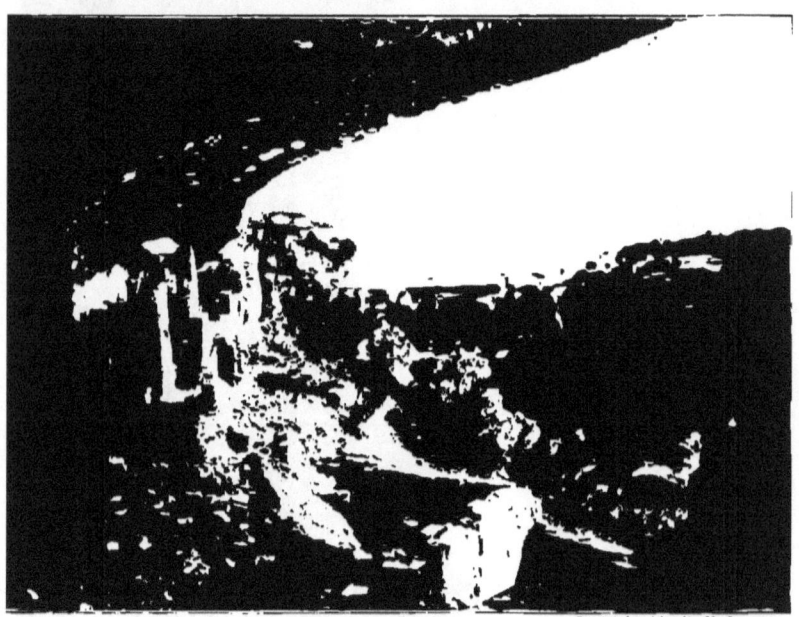

Copyrighted by W. H. Jackson.
CLIFF DWELLERS' HOME, MESA VERDE. RIO GRANDE SOUTHERN R. R.

wouldn't stick out anywhere. The dimensions are something enormous and only equaled by those of the largest of the magnificent palaces that made the White City of the Columbian Exposition so glorious, and which now, alas! have fallen never to rise again. We take great pride in our magnificent Union Depot, and in order that you may know that what I tell you is true here are the comparative figures to support my statements:

St. Pancras, London, England..... 240 x 500 feet.
Union Depot, Frankfort, Germany........... 552 x 600 "
Grand Central Depot, New York.. .... 200 x 750
Union Depot, St. Louis..................... 606 x 820 "

"I think I must have gotten into the very same sleeper, and patronized the very same diner that you girls have grown so enthusiastic about, for I am sure I had the same courteous attention, the same elegant accommodations and the same delightful dinners. But of course, its nonsense to say I

CLIFF PALACE, MESA VERDE, RIO GRANDE SOUTHERN R. R.

had the same car, because, however fast it might go, it couldn't start from Chicago and St. Louis and Omaha and run over three different railroads at the same time. The fact that we are all so absolutely unanimous in our praises of the accommodations that were placed at our command is the best of evidence that we chose wisely in regard to our lines of travel.

"There was little of incident to mark my flitting through

the good old State of Missouri, and whatever happened was no doubt the stuff that dreams are made of, for I must confess I slept soundly during that part of the journey as I left St. Louis in the evening and when I awoke in the morning I found that we had crossed the State line into Kansas. Jennie has delivered a very eloquent lecture on the past, present and future of Nebraska and all I could say about Kansas would be a repetition of her eulogium of her own State with the ex-

BURRO TRAIN TRANSPORTING TIMBERS FOR THE MINES, SILVERTON, COLO

ception that to my mind Kansas is just that much more preferable to Nebraska as it is miles south of it."

You're a true little Southerner," interrupted Jennie.

"Lives there a man with soul so dead,
Who never to himself hath said
This is my own, my native land?"

quoted Julia and that was all the reply she vouchsafed to Jennie's remark. "I never passed a more enjoyable day than the one I spent on the Burlington train *en route* to

OPHIR LOOP. RIO GRANDE SOUTHERN R. R.

THE ROYAL GORGE. GRAND CAÑON OF THE ARKANSAS. ON THE DENVER & RIO GRANDE R. R. HEIGHT OF WALLS, 2,627 FEET. THE CLIMAX OF AWFUL GRANDEUR. LENGTH, 7 MILES. DISTANCE FROM DENVER, 163 MILES.

Denver. I read and I wrote, I looked at the scenery and I sketched and I had a real jolly time with a handsome young commercial traveler who took the sleeper in the morning and got off some time in the afternoon. As he was leaving he said :

"Allow me to thank you for the pleasant time I have had."

"Not at all," said I.

UPPER TWIN LAKES, NEAR LEADVILLE, COLO.   DENVER & RIO GRANDE R. R.

"I'm so glad to have met you," said he.

"Thank you," said I.

"I hope *you* have enjoyed it," said he.

"Now was'nt that cheeky, girls?"

"Oh, very much," said I.

"I'm so glad I succeeded in pleasing you," said he.

"Don't mention it, one is willing to talk to most anybody on the train," said I, and will you believe it girls, the young man got mad and went off in a huff.

"And I don't blame him" exclaimed Joan, "and as for you, it seems to me that you didn't study the scenery to any great extent."

"The proper study of mankind, is man," said Julia, and that seemed to settle the question.

"Our train got into Denver in the morning exactly on time and I found Joan waiting to receive me at the station, and you two girls arrived at about the same time, and all four of us took a carriage and drove to the Brown Palace Hotel and here we all are, happy as larks and ready for future experiences and adventures."

ENTRANCE TO BROWN PALACE.

CHAPTER II.

SUMMER RESORTS AND PICTURESQUE SCENERY.

> Over the mountains of the moon,
> With banter and bravado,
> Rode every knight,
> With sword bedight,
> To land of Eldorado.
> —*Ancient Ballad.*

"NOW that we all are safely met here in Denver, what shall we do next?" This question was put to the quartette of unattended ones by Judith. I say the question was put to the quartette because Judith addressed the query quite as much to herself as to the others.

"I move that we do as the boy said he did when he went after the cows," said Joan.

"And what did the boy say he did?"

"He said, 'First I go to the head of the lane and then I scatter.' We are at the head of the lane, I suggest that we scatter."

"Explain."

"Julia wants to see Clear Creek Cañon and the Loop and I've promised to go with her. You, Judith, want to see Manitou and the Garden of the Gods."

"And I'll go with her," interrupted Jennie.

"Very good," remarked Judith. "Its moved and seconded that we scatter, all in favor say 'yes' and nobody must say no." All voted "yes."

"The question is carried unanimously. Scatter."

The next morning the quartette of merry girls gathered in the ladies' waiting room of the Union depot and purchased

CURRICANTE NEEDLE   BLACK CANON OF THE GUNNISON, ON DENVER & RIO GRANDE R. R.   HEIGHT OF WALLS, 2,500 FEET.   LENGTH OF CANON, 14 MILES.   DISTANCE FROM DENVER, 350 MILES.

Marshall Pass, Mount Ouray in the Distance. Elevation, 10,846 feet. Distance from Denver, 224 miles. Length of Pass, 30 miles.

MONTE CRISTO HOTEL SALIDA, COLO.

tickets for their excursion. Jennie and Judith going to Manitou over the Denver and Rio Grande, and Joan and Julia going to Graymont, the terminus of a branch line of the Denver Union Pacific and Gulf passing through Clear Creek Cañon and over the famous " Loop," with promises to meet at the Brown Palace on the evening of the succeeding day and there to recount the incidents of their outing. The young ladies departed happy in the hope of unalloyed enjoyment. And judging from the tone of their conversation when they met it is quite evident that this hope was not in vain. Behold them gathered the next evening around the table in their cosy parlor at the Brown Palace.

"Isn't Manitou charming?" asked Judith.

"Did you ever see anything so beautiful as the Garden of the Gods?" said Jennie.

"Clear Creek Cañon is just *too* lovely!" murmured Julia.

"And the Loop takes the cake!" exclaimed Joan.

Eagle River Canon, Through Line Denver & Rio Grande R. R. near Red Cliff. Mines and Tramways for Transporting Ore shown in the Engraving. Distance from Denver, 300 miles.

MOUNT OF THE HOLY CROSS. NEAR LEADVILLE. ON THE DENVER & RIO GRANDE R. R.

"Get thee to a bakery," said Judith severely, "slang is not allowed here and don't you forget it."

"Never mind the slang, girls, but tell us about the trip to Manitou," said Julia.

"To start with we had the prettiest car to ride in that I ever saw used on a railroad for just a common everyday car. It had plate glass mirrors, raw silk curtains, mahogany pannels and an ebony porter. I've no doubt there were porcelain bath tubs and a gas range concealed in the car somewhere, for it discounted a *fin de siecle* apartment house in elegance. Don't talk to me about the 'wild and woolly West' after the splendors of that Rio Grande car! The ride of eighty miles along the Front Range to Manitou was a most charming experience. The mountains were in constant view to our right and occasionally we caught a glimpse of the snow-crowned summit of Pike's Peak. Fifty miles West of Denver we came to Palmer

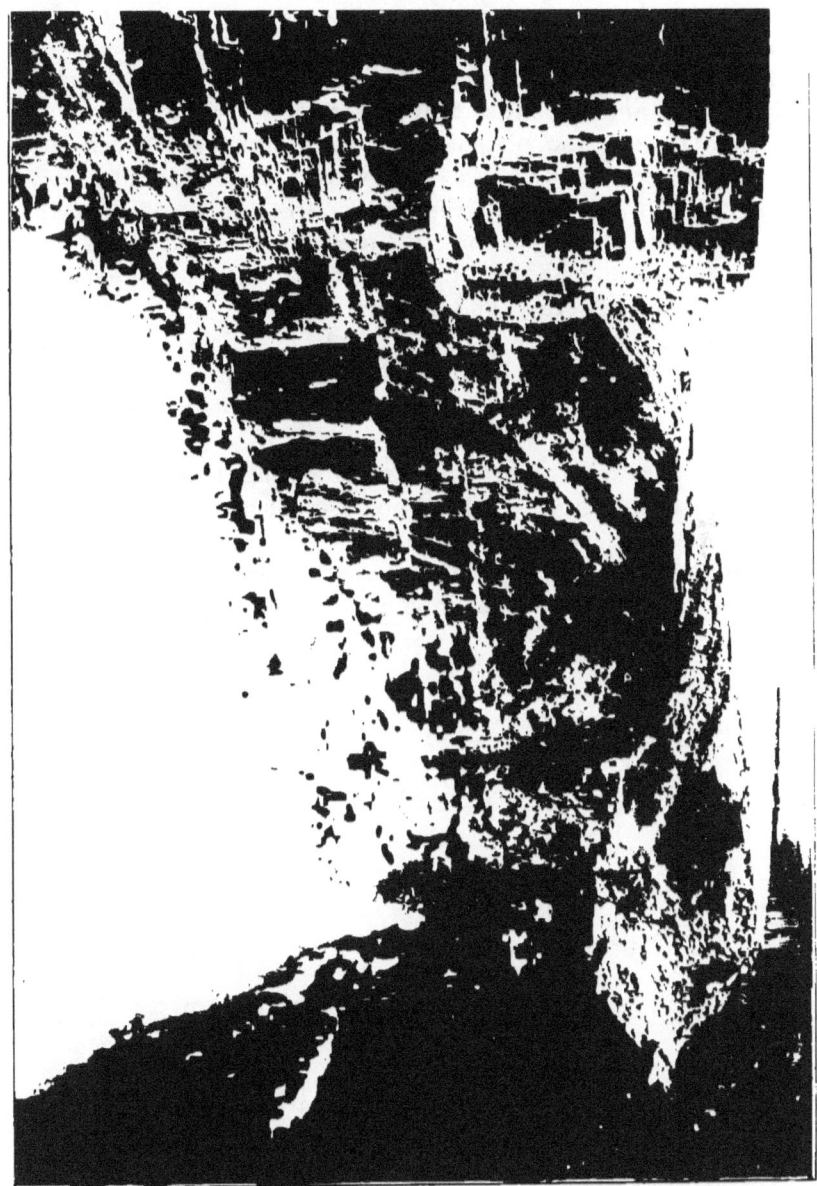

Lake, a beautiful little sheet of water poised on the summit of a spur of hills that extends eastward from the mountains into the plains and which has been given the local title of the Divide. The waters from this lake flow North into the Platte River and South into the Arkansas. Near the station is a pretty little village and here are many handsome summer residences of well to do people who find health, rest and pleasure among the pines and rocky palisades which render the place picturesque and attractive. Here too is located the popular Chatauqua of the West, with a railroad station of its own called Glen Park. Each summer the assembly meets in this romantic spot, the members occupying permanent cottages or temporary abodes as they choose and holding a most instructive session devoted to the study of literary, musical, scientific and religious subjects. A few miles beyond the Divide is Monument Park in which one finds the strangest and most fan-

Second Tunnel, Canon of the Grand River. Denver & Rio Grande R. R.

tastic figures carved from the sandstone through the action of the elements.

"When we reached Colorado Springs, a handsome town of some 12,000 inhabitants, we walked through the magnificent park which lies between the railroad station and the Antlers' Hotel. This park is shaded by innumerable trees and is made beautiful by shaven greensward and beds of carefully nurtured shrubs and flowers. The hotel is a gem of architecture and we found its hospitality fully equal in every respect to its beauty of situation and construction. We took lunch at the Antlers' and engaged a carriage to take us six miles to the westward to Manitou Springs and the Garden of the Gods. We could have gone directly to Manitou by the railroad, or by electric car, but we preferred to drive as we desired to enjoy the view to its fullest extent.

"The mountains towered before us with Pike's Peak in the center and old Cheyenne buttressing the southern terminus of this spur of the Front Range. A good, broad, well-kept road leads from Colorado Springs to Manitou with residences and shops on either side so that it presents quite the appearance of a city street.

"Manitou Springs is the great watering place of the West. Nestled in the little valley among the mountains at the foot of Pike's Peak, sheltered from the winds and lying toward the rising sun, blessed with springs of delicious health giving water, made picturesque by most varied and most lovely scenery and noted as the home of luxury and comfort because of its hotels magnificent in proportion and elegant in equipment, Manitou is indeed an ideal health and pleasure resort. The list of scenic attractions in and around Manitou is almost endless, but in order that you might get some faint idea of what can be seen there, I noted a few of the more prominent places worth visiting, and the distances you will have to drive from the village to reach them:

    Ute Pass and Rainbow Falls...............1½ Miles.
    Garden of the Gods ....3 "
    William's Cañon........... ....½ "

HOTEL COLORADO AND BATH HOUSE, GLENWOOD SPRINGS, COLO. HEALTH AND PLEASURE RESORT. HOTEL AND BATHING POOL AND PAVILION ERECTED AT A COST OF OVER HALF A MILLION DOLLARS.

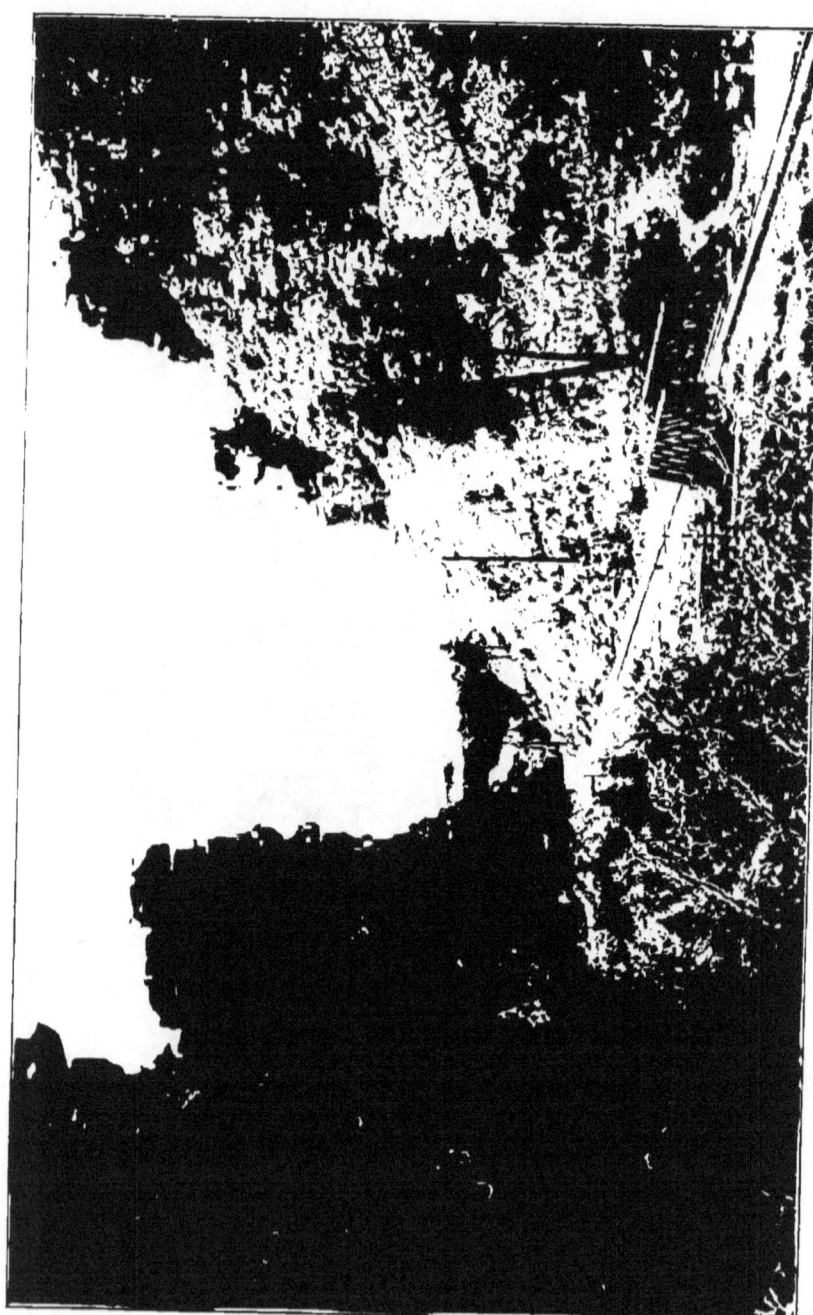

Castle Gate. Rio Grande Western R. R.

Crystal Park............................3	Miles.
Glen Eyrie............................5	"
North Cheyenne Cañon................8½	"
South Cheyenne Cañon.................9	"
Seven Lakes (by horse trail)..........9	"
Summit of Pike's Peak (by cog railroad).....8	"
Monument Park........................9	"

"In the two days which we spent at Manitou we visited Ute Pass, the Garden of the Gods, William's Cañon, South Cheyenne Cañon, Glen Eyrie and Summit of Pike's Peak. They were days of unalloyed delight, and I can't begin to tell you the half of what we saw.

"After we had enjoyed a visit to the springs themselves, which are marvels in their way, and the waters of which are the most delicious I ever drank, we instructed our coachman to drive us to the Garden of the Gods. Leaving Manitou behind us and advancing toward Colorado City, we turned sharply to the left, and found ourselves on the Buena Vista drive, a plainly marked road to the Garden of the Gods. The entrance to the Garden, approaching from Manitou, is through what may not inaptly be called a postern gate as compared with the entrance from the east through the Grand Gateway, made so familiar to eye and mind by photographs and descriptions. Entering from the west, we saw upon our right hand a wall of wind-worn rock crowned with hardy evergreens, while to our left stood the remarkable Balanced Rock, resting its hundreds of tons of weight upon a scanty base of a few feet. Pointing to this rock with his whip, while he reined up his horses with the other hand, the driver said: "See that rock, ladies? Well now that's a curious freak of nature, isn't it?"

"Indeed it is," said I.

"But the most curious thing about it you can't see," continued the driver meditatively.

"Why what is that?" asked Judith innocently.

This was the opportunity our Colorado Jehu was waiting for and assuming an air of critical solemnity he said:

"I don't know whether you'll believe it or not but its a frozen fact. I was the fust one to diskiver it, ma'm, and I find it blamed hard to make any one else believe it, but that's the way with all great diskiveries, look at the man who found out the world waz flat, didn't he have a time! but he knowed it waz so, and everybody knows that it's so now. That rock, ma'm, *revolves clar round on its pedestal onc't every year.*"

"Oh driver!"

"Fact, ma'm I assure you, I'll prove it to you. See that little cross up thar on the side of the rock facing East?"

"Yes."

"Wall if you should come here exactly one year from to-day, you'd find that thar cross in exactly the same place facing East! This proves that the rock has turned clar 'round during the year and brought the cross back to whar it started frum. Get up Charlie, get a move on you Billy," and touching the horses with his whip the driver sent them bowling down the gentle hill into the famous garden.

"Please imagine a vast amphitheatre covering two thousand acres or more, walled in by a chain of tremendous rocks, mostly of red sandstone in beautiful and various shades. As we ride on we see here great hills of rock all tumbled together in every conceivable shape. Proceeding we behold a countless number of the strangest and weirdest figures imaginable, many of them being strikingly natural and correct in shape, resembling men, women, castles and many creatures of both land and sea. The crowning wonder of this home of wonders is the colossal eastern gateway towering more than three hundred feet above the roadway on each hand, leaving barely enough space to admit of the passage of a carriage.

"Imagine rocks rising straight out of the ground many feet wide and not more than two or three feet thick, towering three hundred feet or more, all of a beautiful red sandstone. Here are the Cathedral Spires, while yonder upon a mighty rock, as if viewing the garden, stands the "Indian Maid." On every hand one sees towers, buttresses, pinnacles, slender spires and minarets of flashing coral color, but as we turn a projection we see a reef of rock, white as the driven snow. Imagine the contrast! Further on there is a beautiful mingling of various colors and tints in mighty strata of rock. Truly this seems to have been the playground of the Titans, the Garden of the Gods.

From the Garden we drove to South Cheyenne Cañon.

LONG BRIDGE OVER THE GRAND RIVER, AT GRAND JUNCTION, COLO.
RIO GRANDE WESTERN R. R.

This is a cleft in the heart of Old Cheyenne Mountain. We entered with a feeling of reverence and followed a winding path over rocks, between tall evergreens and across the rushing current of a brook, the waters of which boil and foam down the narrow channel. In this deep hollow only the noonday sun shines. Going up the cañon with the roar of the waters ahead and the winding path before us, the lofti-

PROVO FALLS, UTAH. RIO GRANDE WESTERN R. R.

ness and savage wildness of the walls catch only a dizzying glance, but coming out their tops seem to touch the heavens and their height to be measureless. The eye can hardly take in the vast height, and with the afternoon sun touching only the extreme tops, one realizes in what crevice and fissure of the rocks the cañon winds. The narrow gorge ends in a round well of granite, down one side of which leaps, slides, foams and rushes the Seven Falls a series of cascades—seven in line, pouring the water from the melted snow above into this cup.

"Above the waterfall, on the eastward slope of Cheyenne Mountain, is the grave of one of America's truest poets and most remarkable women, 'H. H.' Here the late Helen Hunt Jackson lies asleep among the scenes she loved. Cheyenne cañon has henceforth for me a profounder meaning—its unexampled beauty being supplemented by a sacred and tender memory.

> Oh, Cheyenne cañon! in thy dim defiles,
> Where gloams the light, as through cathedral aisles,
> Where flash and fall bright waters, pure as air,
> Where wild birds brood, wild blossoms bloom, and where
> The wind sings anthems through the darkling trees,
> A presence breathes the tenderest melodies.
>
> Songs that the finer ear of poets feel
> But do not hear, ethereal chords that steal
> Upon the soul as fragrance of the flowers,
> Unseen, unknown, from undiscovered bowers,
> Enwraps the senses with a deep delight,
> Pure as the stars and tender as the night.
>
> For here in Nature's arms there lies asleep
> One who loved nature with a passion deep,
> Who knew her language and who read her book,
> Who sang her music, which the bird, the brook,
> The winds, the woods, the mountains and the seas
> Chant ever, in commingling harmonies.
>
> Oh, Cheyenne cañon! through thy dim defiles
> The music floats as through cathedral aisles;
> The singer silent, but the song is heard
> In sigh of wind and carolling of bird,

All these the poet's melodies prolong,
For nature now sings o'er her loved one's song.

"Glen Eyrie was the next place of interest that we visited after beholding the beauties of Cheyenne Cañon. The drive was one of pleasant interest, seven or eight miles to the northward among low lying hills and past the great gateway of the Garden of the Gods. The Glen contains the summer residence of the projector and first President of the Denver and Rio Grande railroad. It is a wilderness of beauty hidden

CAÑON OF GRAND RIVER, RIO GRANDE WESTERN R. R.

between the rose tinted rocks of Queen's Cañon. Trees and shrubs covered with clambering vines, make cool and shaded resorts for singing birds, and meandering through is a babbling mountain brook. Tall columnar rocks, similar to those in the Garden of the Gods abound, the most striking of which bears the title of the Major Domo. The summer residence is surrounded by handsome lawns and gardens, and the whole presents a restful retreat from the toil and turmoil of the work-a day world.

"After our visit to Glen Eyrie we returned to Colorado Springs, driving across the Mesa, which is a high tableland as level as a floor, extending from the Garden of the Gods to within a mile or two of the Springs. The view from the Mesa was most inspiring, embracing the whole range of mountains from Long's to Pike's Peak and thence as far south as the Spanish peaks, over one hundred miles distant.

"We took dinner at the Antlers, which was served with all the elegance and perfection of detail that one might expect to

LOOKOUT ROCKS, CANON OF GRAND RIVER.   RIO GRANDE WESTERN R. R.

find in the first-class hostelries of the great metropolitan cities of the East or Europe. We spent the night in this charming hotel, and I assure you, girls, that for comfort and elegance the Antlers is *facile princeps*."

"Translate," exclaimed Joan, with the air of a tutor in Latin.

"She means 'out of sight,'" said Julia.

"I don't mean anything of the kind," replied Judith se-

HALF TUNNEL, CANON OF THE GRAND RIVER. RIO GRANDE WESTERN.

verely, "except that everything unpleasant was out of sight at the Antlers."

"Go on with your story or you'll never get through," said Joan.

"The next morning we walked about Colorado Springs and found it a most beautiful little city made up of unusually handsome homes, and we learned that it was considered the most aristocratic and intelligent town in the West. Very many rich people live there, and society is of the best. After our walk we took the electric line to Manitou, bent on ascending the great peak.

"Pike's Peak had challenged our curiosity ever since we beheld it from the train, a faint blue cloud on the horizon, long before we reached Denver. Now we were about to accept this challenge and achieve the conquest of this monarch of the Front Range. The cogwheel road from Manitou to the summit made our victory an easy task, substituting an element of novelty to take the place of that element of adventure which spiced the ascent on horseback in former days. The road is constructed in a most substantial manner, the ballast being of rock and the rails of the best of steel. Between the rails, in the centre of the track, extends the cogway, into which the cogwheels of the engine press, held in place by the many tons weight of that great machine.

"In making the ascent the engine pushes the coaches loaded with passengers up the steep incline, and in descending backs down, holding the train from making too rapid progress under the influence of gravity. The conductor explained all these matters to me very kindly before we began the upward journey, but aside from the fact that I was firmly convinced of the perfect safety of the trip, I can't remember the technicalities. Experience added to my confidence, and I am perfectly satisfied that an accident is an event that has been rendered practically impossible on this marvelous, mountain-climbing road.

"We boarded the train at the station, which is near the famous Iron Ute Spring, and were soon making a steady and comparatively rapid ascent of the hills that lie at the foot of the great Peak. The track mounts steadily up the steep side of the ravine, so narrow that the wall of rock had to be blasted away to give room for the road. Sometimes a great shoulder of granite seems to cut off the track altogether, but the way opens as if by magic, sometimes a bridge at a dizzy height spans a chasm and echoes to the tread of our iron horse. A thick fog fills the chasm, out of it at times peer rocks so huge that from a single one could be built castles or capitols. Could we but have heard the thunder of their fall when they crushed down the steeps and tore away forests in their path! As we ascend, the view to the eastward over the plains widens and a glorious prospect meets our vision. The summit of the peak presents an area of about seventy acres of granite blocks, varying in size from that of a freight car to that of a pea. Below us are the clouds and we

Temple Block, Salt Lake City, showing Mormon Temple, the Great Tabernacle and Assembly Hall.

THE KNUTSFORD HOTEL, SALT LAKE CITY, UTAH.

watch the sheen of the sunbeams on their billowy upper surfaces. Midway down the mountain slope they sway as do the waves of a wind swept sea. Suddenly like a drawn curtain, they roll away, and as from the height of another planet we look upon the majestic globe beneath. Mountains no longer rise but lie crouching at our feet, forests great and grim, become simply dark shadows in the distance. A city is abridged to the dimensions of a single square and a great river becomes a sinuous line of darker green on the lighter verdure of the distant prairies.

"After this vision from the top of the world, we felt that the acme of grandeur had been reached, and with a sigh over the glory that we must leave behind us, we returned to our car and made the descent. Taking an afternoon train from Colorado Springs, we reached Denver in time for dinner.

"And now you know all about our journey to the Springs and what we saw there. Tell us what you saw."

SALTAIR, SOUTH FRONT OF PAVILION, THE NOTED BATHING RESORT, SALT LAKE. RIO GRANDE WESTERN R. R.

AMERICAN NATURAL GAS AND OIL CO.'S WELLS. OUTPUT 12,000,000 CUBIC FEET DAILY. GREAT SALT LAKE, UTAH.

Joan looked at Julia and Julia looked at Joan, each awaiting for the other to speak. Finally Julia said: "I think Joan ought to be the orator on this occasion."

"Why?" asked Joan.

"For three reasons; first, you live in Denver, and are familiar with the subject under discussion; second, I have been the narrator on another occasion; thirdly, *because*."

"The last reason settles it, I'll tell the story," said Joan, smiling.

"The trip from Denver to the Loop is a favorite excursion with our people during the summer months. Every Sunday long trains loaded with excursionists pull out of the Union Depot bound for Clear Creek Cañon and the Loop. Strangers in Colorado are always anxious to see the wonders that exist upon this branch of the Denver, Union Pacific & Gulf Railway, which, aside from being a great freight route

GARFIELD BEACH AND GREAT SALT LAKE, UTAH, FROM THE CAVE, ON UNION PACIFIC SYSTEM.

CASTILLA SPRINGS HEALTH RESORT, SPANISH FORK CANON.
RIO GRANDE WESTERN R. R.

to ,and from the gold, silver and coal mines, is also a truly remarkable scenic line.

"The little town of Golden was soon reached, and just beyond we entered Clear Creek Cañon. At Forks Creek the line branches, one track running up to the famous mining towns of Central City and Black Hawk, and the other to Georgetown, Graymont and the Loop. On the latter is Idaho Springs, a famous health resort in the heart of the mountains.

MAIN STREET, OGDEN, UTAH, ON UNION PACIFIC SYSTEM.

"Clear Creek Cañon is about an hour's ride from Denver. The railroad until it reaches the foothills, runs through fields as green and past farmhouses as pleasant as any of which the older States can boast.

"The cañon is a marvelous cleft, worn through the solid rock by Clear Creek, dashing and roaring near the track, which crosses it at short intervals. Its sides, time-worn in a thousand grotesque forms, rise from 500 to 1,500 feet, making the sky appear a mere narrow strip of the deepest blue. In places there are great side cañons through which rivulets come silvering down as the sunlight strikes across the somber shadows. Trees grow thick in places, and crown a portion of the heights.

"After leaving Georgetown we were on the *qui vive* for we knew that we were approaching the famous 'loop'. Soon the train began a steep ascent among the hills and the curves became shorter and more abrupt. The way for the track was carved through solid rock and skirted the sides of mountains that lost their crests in snow. In the valley below we could see the flashing waters of Clear Creek. Past Devil's Gate and Bridal Veil Falls the engine labored upward. Looking directly above we saw a railroad track on a high iron bridge overspanning the track almost at right angles, but in the form of a crescent." Julia, wonderingly inquired:

"'What road is that above?'

"In a few moments we were on the bridge, and Julia, looking down, caught sight of another track and asked: 'What road is that below?'

"Then I condescended to explain that they were both one and the same track. From the top six tracks apparently belonging to different lines were seen. Then Julia realized that she had just ridden over the famous loop—one of four in existence. There is one on the Southern Pacific Railroad, one in Switzerland, and one in the Andes of South America, but this is the most complex of them all. The bridge we crossed is 300 feet long and 86 feet high. From Georgetown it can be seen one way nestled in the mountains; looking at it from the other way there seems to be nothing but a confusion of tracks.

"It was a remarkable climb from here to the Big Fill, which is 76 feet high, but the curve is too sharp to admit of a bridge, and comes nearer being a duplication of 'The Loop.' Georgetown was still in sight beyond the three parallel tracks of 'The Loop.' Looking down the final curve we saw a wealth of track, but it dodged hither and

Liberty Cap. Mammoth Hot Springs. Yellowstone Park reached via Union Pacific System.

AMES MONUMENT, SHERMAN, WYO., ON THE UNION PACIFIC SYSTEM.

thither, no portion seemingly having any special relation to its neighbor; occasionally the entire trackage came into view at once. After passing 'The Loop' and Silver Plume, Graymont, the terminus of the railway was reached.

"Our return to Denver was made enjoyable by the renewed opportunity it gave us to study the beauty and grandeur of the marvelous cañon down which rush and swirl the waters of Clear Creek."

"And what did you do to-day?" asked Judith.

"Visited places of interest in Denver," replied Julia, "and a very pleasant day we have had too. We went to one of the many great smelters which are to be found in the suburbs and got some idea how gold and silver are extracted from the unpromising rocks which are thrown into the glowing furnaces. We strolled through the parks, took a peep into the Tabor Grand Opera House and the Broadway Theater, and found both of them models of elegance and beauty.

Shopped a little, and I was surprised at the size of the leading stores and the extent and fine quality of the goods displayed. My attention was attracted to a tablet let into the wall in front of H. H. Tammen's curiosity store, where souvenirs of the mountains, Indian relics, mounted animal heads, and a thousand and one curious bits of bric-a-brac were on sale and exhibition, but the tablet was the thing that first attracted my attention. It bore the inscription:

> THIS TABLET IS
> PLACED JUST ONE MILE
> ABOVE THE SEA.

"I found the business part of the city well built, tall blocks of brick and stone much in evidence, streets well paved with asphalt and everything denoting metropolitan

GIANT'S TEA KETTLE, GREEN RIVER, WYO., ON UNION PACIFIC SYSTEM.

WITCHES ROCKS, WEBER CANON, UTAH, ON UNION PACIFIC.

thrift and prosperity. The residence parts of the city surprised me because of the elegance of the houses and the charm given them by spacious lawns and carefully nurtured ornamental trees and shrubs. The streets are rendered cool and pleasant by rows of elms, maples and cottonwoods, and I don't remember even one house built of wood, pressed brick and many varieties of beautiful colored stone being used exclusively. In a word, Denver impresses me as being one of the handsomest cities I have ever seen."

"Not excepting your own St. Louis?"

"I said *one* of the handsomest."

"Oh! Now what shall we do to-morrow?" asked Judith.

"To-morrow, methinks I hear Horatio say to-morrow" quoted Joan, "Go to, there is no such word save in the ———"

"Good night," exclaimed the other girls, drowning the rest of the quotation and departing tired but happy for a night's sound sleep.

CHAPTER III.

OVER THE GREAT DIVIDE TO GLENWOOD.

> "Merrily through the hills we go,
> Over the mountains crowned with snow,
> Into the valleys green below,
> Merrily, merrily, Oh!
>
> —*Song of the Cabalero.*

NEXT morning after a hearty breakfast, the excellence of which was fully appreciated by the young ladies, for they did not belong to the class of romantic creatures that are "too bright and good for human nature's daily food," a council of war was held and the question of what to do next was propounded for discussion.

"Of course," said Judith, "we are all agreed that Salt Lake City shall be the next stage in our journey, but there are two trunk lines to that place from Denver and the question is which shall we take."

"The Union Pacific is good enough for me," said Jennie.

"I should like to go by the Denver and Rio Grande," said Julia.

"I am willing to go either way," said Joan.

"My vote is for the Rio Grande," remarked Judith, "and I am in favor of this line for several reasons. I'll give only one, however, and that is, the ticket I bought in Chicago reads over that line."

"And by a curious coincidence mine reads over the Union Pacific," exclaimed Jennie.

"Mine is via the Rio Grande," remarked Julia, demurely.

"It doesn't take much acumen to discover why you girls prefer certain lines," laughed Joan. "I'm the only unpreju-

THE STAR GEYSER, YELLOWSTONE NATIONAL PARK, WYO., UNION PACIFIC SYSTEM.

GREEN RIVER, BUTTES, WYO.   UNION PACIFIC SYSTEM.

diced one in the party, for I havn't bought my ticket yet. As Julia and Judith are booked over the Rio Grande and Jennie over the Union Pacific, I decide to go with Jennie and suggest that we meet at the Knutsford Hotel in Salt Lake City and there recount our experiences."

This arrangement proved satisfactory and the young travelers meeting as agreed upon, with mutual enthusiasm told the story of their adventures.

The proprietor of the Knutsford took special pains to make the young ladies comfortable and as a result they found themselves supplied with a very handsome suite of apartments with a most cosy and homelike parlor in which to hold their symposium.

"Who speaks first?" asked Joan.

"Judith, of course," said Jennie.

"Why Judith and why of course?" asked Judith.

"Oh because," said Jennie.

YELLOWSTONE CANON. YELLOWSTONE NATIONAL PARK. REACHED VIA UNION PACIFIC SYSTEM.

PULPIT TERRACES, MAMMOTH HOT SPRINGS, YELLOWSTONE NATIONAL PARK. REACHED VIA UNION PACIFIC SYSTEM.

"Carried," said Joan, "and there is no appeal from the decision of the chair." Then Judith began by saying "We have been on the roof of the world, we have looked down on the clouds, we have been in the nethermost depths and have seen the stars at midday."

"That's nothing," interrupted Joan, "we saw the *sun* at midday, did'nt we Jennie?"

"Yes, and the stars at midnight," replied Jennie.

"If I'm to be interrupted—" began Judith.

"You're *not* to be interrupted," said Joan, "only that star business rather star-tled me."

"A fine is recorded against Joan," said Julia sententiously.

"Wherefore?"

"You made a pun."

"I did'nt mean to."

"Double the fine for not knowing it was loaded. Proceed, Judith."

"We took the standard gauge line of the Rio Grande from Denver to Salt Lake because that is the regular transcontinental route. We could have gone via the narrow gauge branch, over Marshall Pass, the highest railroad pass on the continent, and through the famous black Cañon in which towers the Currecanti Needle, and onward to Grand Junction, but, as I have said, we preferred the great through route by

GREAT SHOSHONE FALLS, IDAHO, REACHED VIA UNION PACIFIC SYSTEM.

way of Leadville, Glenwood Springs and thence to Grand Junction.

"The Rio Grande line to Salt Lake and Ogden extends southward from Denver through Colorado Springs to Pueblo, a distance of 120 miles. From the latter point it swerves westward, and with many meanderings, maintains an average of westward coursing until Salt Lake City is reached. We have discussed the beauties of Manitou and its surroundings, so it is not necessary to say more on that subject. As the train entered the northern suburbs of Pueblo we noticed the domes and columns of a very large and handsome building. Inquiring we learned that we were getting a glimpse of the famous Mineral Palace. This building is extremely unique in its architecture and contains, perhaps, the most complete and certainly the most attractive collection of mineral specimens in the world. Within its magnificent spaces are housed thousands of choice samples of gold, silver, iron, coal, mar-

GREAT SHOSHONE FALLS, IDAHO, LOOKING DOWN THE CANON.
REACHED VIA UNION PACIFIC SYSTEM.

ble, onyx and innumerable curious and valuable substances that are taken from the hills of Colorado. There is a vast rotunda and a hall for lectures and musical entertainments, with an ample stage. One of the curious ornaments of this auditorium is a statue made of coal, which has been humorously christened "Old King Cole."

"Pueblo is the second city of Colorado, with a population of 50,000. Here are located the great steel works of the Colorado Coal and Iron Co., second to no plant of the kind in the world. There are also a number of smelters for gold and silver ores and many other large manufacturing enterprises.

At Florence, thirty-two miles west of Pueblo, we broke our journey to take a run up the new Florence and Cripple Creek Railroad to make a flying visit to Colorado's great gold camp. Florence is the site of petroleum wells and the tall

CASTLE CRAGS.   SOUTHERN PACIFIC R. R.

derricks remind one of the palmy days of Oil City and Titusville. The town is "booming," as the westerners say, new buildings going up and business rushing. Smelting plants and reduction works, to treat the gold ores of the Cripple Creek district, are in operation and in process of erection. The Florence and Cripple Creek Railroad is a scenic line as well as a great freight route. Extending through deep cuts and cañons among the mountains, a distance of forty miles from

El Capitan, Yosemite Valley, Cal. Reached via the Southern Pacific R. R.

Florence to the town of Cripple Creek, it presents scenes of most striking interest and illustrates the energy and pluck of railroad builders in the great West. Among the many curious things we saw on this trip, was a great cut in the hills which we were informed had been thrown out by a single blast. Our attention was also attracted to a pine tree of good proportions growing from a split in an immense upheaved rock.

"What can I tell you about Cripple Creek? If I should

UMBRELLA TREE, PASADENA, CAL.

say that they mined gold there with a plow and scraper, I should tell you the truth, but not the whole truth. There are mines that are worked like open quarries, mines that are like sand hills full of gold dust, mines that are tunnels and shafts in solid rocks, mines of every kind and character, but the one thing that is true is that Cripple Creek and its environs, including Victor, abound in gold, plenty of it and of very great richness. I can't begin to tell you half the wonders I saw. If I should say that the output of Cripple Creek is $25,000 a day for every day in the year, including Sundays, I wouldn't get it high enough, and if I got high enough for to-day, it wouldn't be high enough for to-morrow. If I were to tell you about riding into a boiling, seething, roaring, brand new mining camp in a Pullman palace car, I wouldn't be telling you half the wonders of the Florence and Cripple Creek railroad. You must allow your imagination full play and you'll then fall far short of the truth.

DATE PALM, PASADENA CAL.

"We returned to Florence and resumed our journey toward Salt Lake, so filled with wonder and astonishment that the peaceful scenery of the valley along the Arkansas river, up whose bank we were proceeding, came like a benediction. Orchards abounding in apple, peach, cherry and all kinds of fruit trees, vineyards rich in growing grapes, meadows green with alfalfa, fields made lovely with nodding corn, cosy cottages nestled among shade trees, presented a scene of sylvan beauty and content.

"Cañon City was soon reached, a charming little residence town, the center of the fruit growing section in this part of Colorado. There are medicinal springs here and a sanitarium for invalids. There is one honor belonging to Cañon City that no other town in the State can claim, and that is the fact that it stands guard over the gateway to the Grand Cañon of the Arkansas, the most magnificent, awe-inspiring and tremendous natural wonder that can be found in all the Rocky Mountain Range.

"There are some things that can only be known through experience, that can never be described, that defy analysis and that make us understand how weak are words when feeling holds full sway. The ride through the Grand Cañon is one of those experiences. No language can describe it, no painting simulate it, nothing can suggest its grandeur unless the soul, alive to music, may catch some hint of its grandeur in the 'Ocean Symphony.' For the distance of a mile or two above Cañon City the bluffs of the Arkansas river grow gradually more sharp and precipitous until they begin to tower like cyclopean walls on each side of the track. The road winds in and out, following the current of the river until all at once a great buttress of solid rock seems to stand directly in front of us as if to prevent further progress, but with a quick turn the engine swerves around the obstruction and we find ourselves within the magic precincts of the Grand Cañon. Here it is that we realize the inadequacy of words to picture the grandeur of the scene which lies before us. The walls of the cañon rise in precipitous reaches to such a dizzy height that the eye with difficulty grasps the stupendous spectacle. The road lies along the base of the great cliff, with the river roaring and rushing by its side, and so narrow is the way that in many places tunnels have been cut through projecting rocks and in other instances the roadway has been blasted from the solid granite. At one point the walls approach each other so closely that there is no

Market Street, San Francisco, Cal.

space left for both the river and the road and a bridge has been constructed lengthwise with the stream, suspended from iron trusses let into the rocks on either hand. Here the cliffs extend above our heads in towering majesty to the height of over half a mile, and the sky is a ribbon of deep blue in which the stars appear no matter how young or old the day may be. This is the Royal Gorge, the climax of grandeur!

THE PRIZE TALLYHO, THE RAYMOND, PASADENA, CAL.

"For nine miles this great gorge extends through the Front Range and for every mile of this wonderous cañon there are new and startling combinations of beauty and magnificence. But it's useless for me to try to describe what I saw. The only way to realize its grandeur is to go and see it yourself. Beyond the western entrance to the cañon, the road still follows the river and we had charming views of quiet beauty, which served as a foil to the awe-inspiring scenery of the grand cañon. Soon the pretty town of Salida is reached and here we paused for a space long enough to secure a surprisingly good meal at the Monte Christo Hotel, a handsome structure adjoining the railroad station. And right here I want to say that the Denver and Rio Grand hotels and eating houses deserve the highest praise. The Union Depot Hotel at Pueblo, the Monte Christo, at Salida, and the eating houses at Leadville, Cimarron, Minturn and Grand Junction, are all of a high degree of excellence. The food is well

THE RAYMOND, PASADENA, CALIFORNIA.

cooked, promptly served and of the best quality, while everything is scrupulously neat and clean.

"From Salida, one branch of the line extends to Grand Junction via Marshall Pass, as I have already told you, and the main line reaches the same point by way of Leadville and Glenwood Springs, we going as you know by the latter route, following the Arkansas River almost at its source. Beyond Salida we passed through the upper valley of the Arkansas. On our right to the northward, sweeps the great South Park, one of those peculiar mountain valleys, a chain of which extends from North to South in the Rocky Range and known respectively as North Park, Middle Park, South Park, San Louis Valley and the Montezuma Valley. These parks are vast grass-grown plains surrounded by mountains and most of them have a larger area than that of some of the Eastern states.

"The scenery between Salida and Leadville is very varied,

MAGNOLIA AVENUE, RIVERSIDE, CALIFORNIA.

giving us a glimpse of placer mining along the banks of the river, and of hill, valley and mountain including the famous Collegiate Range with its lofty peaks known by the titles of Yale, Harvard and Princeton. There are mines among all these mountains and the gold and silver prospectors have here a rich field in which to labor.

"Leadville is a marvelous city of about 20,000 inhabitants. Thirty years ago it was a famous gold camp, and the placers of California gulch yielded millions of dollars worth of the yellow dust. Ten years ago it was a great silver camp and gained the title of Leadville, because of the lead bearing silver ore which was found there in marvelous abundance. To-day, it is once more a gold camp, and is excelling its early history in the production of gold. A wonderful fact about Leadville is that it is situated more than 10,000 feet above sea level, and in this respect is unique among the cities of the world. The wealth that has been taken from the mines of Leadville, and produced from her varied business enterprises is something stupendous; and with the new impetus received from the recent gold discoveries, the past history of the city, brilliant though it be, bids fair to be eclipsed by its future achievements. The town is completely surrounded by high, snow-crowned mountain peaks, and the view is transcendently beautiful.

"Beyond Leadville the road plunges into the heart of the mountains, passing under the historic Tennessee Pass by means of a tunnel. This is the Great Divide of the continent, and when we emerge from the darkness of the tunnel we see that the streams are all running westward instead of towards the East, and we know that we are now on the Pacific slope. Beyond the pass a short distance, the polite Pullman conductor warns us that we are approaching the only point on this line from which we can get a good view of the Mount of the Holy Cross, so we take possession of the rear platform and with eager eyes watch for this wonderful spectacle. A little valley opens to the left, and looking upward toward the southeast, we see the summit of this marvelous mountain swinging into view, and soon we behold the emblem of the Christian faith resting on the granite bosom of the peak. The cross is perfect in its proportions, being caused by deposits of snow in a vertical cañon, and on a transverse ledge. This snow, owing to its sheltered position, does not melt, while the winter mantel on the rest of the mountain disappears under the influence of the warm spring sunshine. The sight is thrilling, no matter what may be the faith of the observer, and is worth a journey across the continent to behold.

"Following the westward flowing waters of the Eagle River we reach Red Cliff, a mining town of no great size but of considerable importance in mining circles because of the rich silver lodes which are found here and especially along the crest of Battle Mountain. This mountain frowns down upon the road as it makes its sinuous way through Eagle River Cañon, and the shafthouses of the miners could be seen perched like the nests of eagles on the beetling cliffs above us as we whirled onward between walls of granite whose summits reached at altitude of 2,000 feet. We were interested in observing the wire tramways leading like spiderwebs from the shafthouses, so high above us, down to the track, and we learned that the freight cars employed in carrying ore are loaded easily and expeditiously by means of these tramways. The scenery of Eagle River Cañon is very beautiful, made softer in effect by the presence of abundant and umbrageous pines. Beyond the cañon we enter the Eagle River Valley, a lovely vale shut in by Alpine hills——"

"Yes, we know all about the 'lovely vale,' don't quote Claude Melnotte's rhapsody to us," interrupted Jennie.

"I know of nothing that describes it better," continued Judith, "but if you object I'll drop the quotation. The valley is made pleasant and fruitful by a happy and industrious people, who possess wide acres which are carefully and intelligently cultivated. The Eagle River is a clear and sparkling stream abounding in trout and making the valley fertile with its waters. Rushing along at the rate of thirty to forty miles an hour, the train soon traverses the length of Eagle River Valley and the scenery begins to change its aspect. The farther bank of the Eagle River is now a mass of black scoria, the deposit from some volcano whose fires were extinguished long ages ago. The phenomenon is striking and at once attracts our attention. Tall cliffs arise on each side of the track and off to our right we see the junction of the Eagle with the Grand River and the sparkling

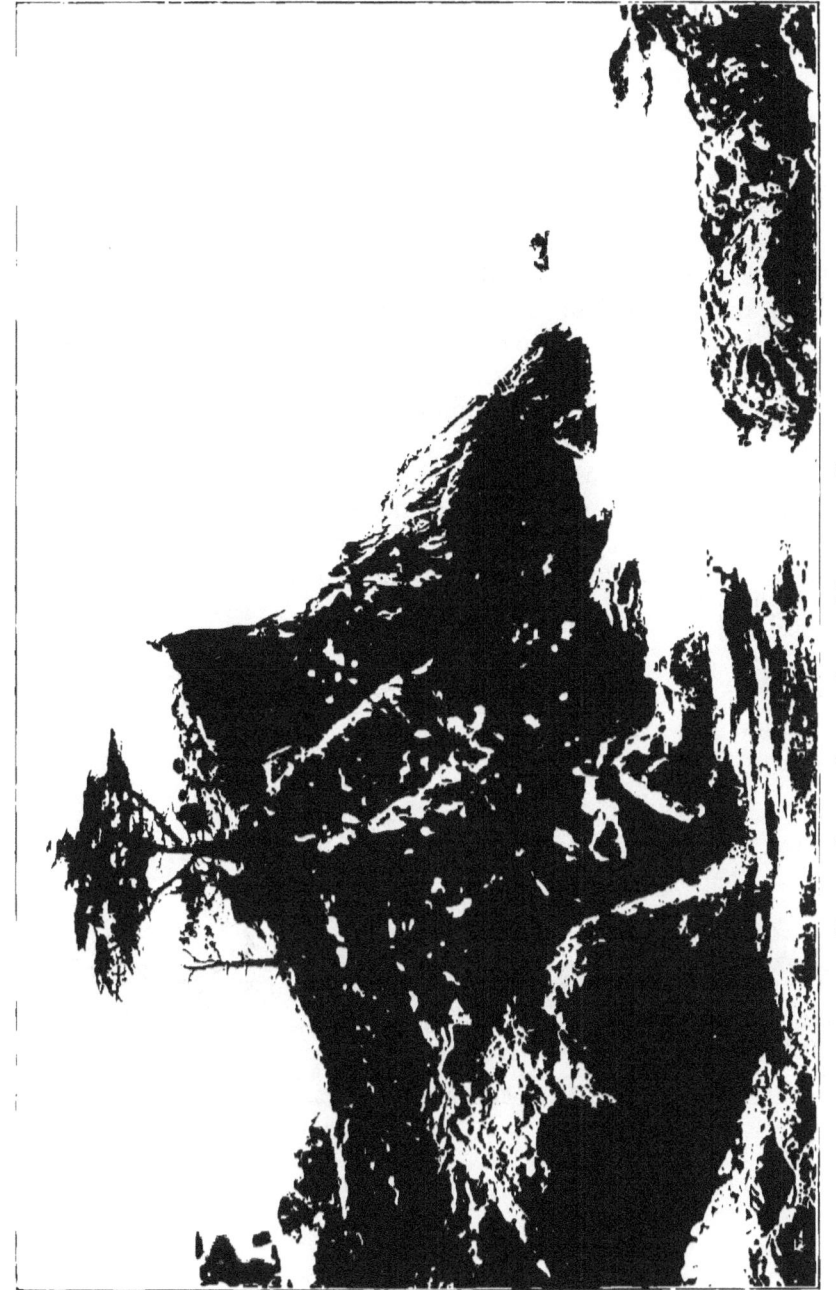

Midway Point, Cypress Drive, Monterey, California.

current of the former is lost in the turbulent flood of the latter. Then wonders in rock-piling are beheld, towers and pinnacles, domes, minarets and obelisks arise, vast walls of vari-colored stone hem us in and we realize that we have entered the noble Cañon of the Grand River. This Cañon is longer than that of the Arkansas, more varied, more interesting, but less awful, less sublime. It abounds in surprises. It has moments of arabesque beauty followed by moments of awful sublimity. The walls in some places soar to a height of 2,500 feet and seem to tangle their granite fingers in the clouds. Ample opportunity is given to study the infinite variety of this great gorge for it is many miles in length, but finally the train plunges into darkness and tunnel No. 1 is reached. A few moments after it has been passed we enter tunnel No. 2, and shortly tunnel No. 3 lies before us. This is the longest of them all and when once more the bright sunlight reappears we see before us the famous health resort of the Rocky Mountains, Glenwood Springs.

CHAPTER IV.

ONWARD TO THE CITY OF THE SAINTS

>'I met a maid in serge arrayed,
>She bore a cross and psalter.
>Her eyes were bright as is the light
>Upon the sacred altar.
>Fair maid, cried I, pray tell me why,
>And answer me in pity,
>Why do you go? She answered low.
>I seek the Holy City."
>
>*Ballad of the Crusader.*

ALADDINS PALACE would not have surprised me more than did the splendid edifice of the Hotel Colorado supplemented by the magnificence of the vast bathing house. Nearly a million of dollars have been invested in these two buildings and the contiguous improvements.

"The hotel is in the Italian style, the Villa Medicis in Rome having given inspiration for its central motive, which consists of two towers with connecting loggias, offering fine outlooks over valley, mountain and river. It is constructed of Peach Blow colored stone and Roman brick. Its dimensions are 224 feet across the front and 260 feet from front to rear. The hotel is built around three sides of a large court, 124 feet square. In locating the building, advantage was taken of the natural slope of the ground, thus enabling the court to be terraced and adorned with fountains, paths, grass plats and beds of flowers.

"The immense hot spring which pours its fervid waters into the river is one of the most wonderful of the many wonderful things to be seen at Glenwood. I was informed that every sixty seconds, 2000 gallons of water, at a tempera-

Mt. Shasta, California, altitude 14,440 feet. Reached via Shasta Route, Southern Pacific R. R.

ture of 120 degrees Fahrenheit, gush out of the earth and pour into the big bathing pool which covers more than an acre of ground and varies in depth from three and one-half to five and one-half feet. In winter as well as summer the bath is in the highest degree enjoyable, the temperature of the great body of water being from 93° to 98° Fahrenheit, being cooled by water from the river. In the midst of the hot waters a fountain of cold water throws its grateful spray, forming a delightful shower bath. The bath house was a revelation to us for we had no idea that we should find so much of luxury and elegance here in the heart of the Rocky Mountains. Its walls are of solid masonry, the beautiful Peach Blow sandstone being the material used. It is a large building, set in a charming park, with terraced lawns and flower bordered walks and drives. There are forty-four bath rooms, with a dressing and lounging room for each bath room, and all are large, well lighted and well ventilated. The building contains also a ladies' parlor, physician's office, smoking and reading rooms, reception rooms, etc., all of which are elegantly furnished. It is lighted by electricity. It can readily be inferred that Glenwood Springs is a very popular health and pleasure resort, possessing grand scenery, an altitude of 5,200 feet, a sheltered position in a sunny valley and marvelous hot springs, of great curative properties. A branch of the Denver & Rio Grande Railroad extends through the mountains from this point to Aspen, a distance of 41 miles, one of the richest mining towns in the West, a handsome city of 6,500 population, situated amidst the grandest of scenery.

"From Glenwood Springs the train rolled rapidly down a fertile and picturesque valley along the course of the Grand River. On one side the hills hedged in the view, while on the other the valley extended back to the picturesque Book Cliffs, whose ramparts of multi-colored rock, carved into an infinite variety of form by the action of wind and frost and water, rose into view. We enjoyed the delightfully varied scenery until the porter announced Grand Junction and in-

SPEARFISH CAÑON, ON THE BURLINGTON ROUTE.

formed us that the train would stop there for half an hour.

"We took advantage of the stop to stroll on the station platform and enjoy the balmy air and the bright sunshine. The Pullman conductor, who had proved exceedingly kind, approached us and said, 'Excuse me, but if you would like to know anything about Colorado scenery, or railroads, or politics, or literature, that gentleman, I was just speaking to, can tell you all about them. He's going to Salt Lake in our Pullman.'

"'Who is he,' I asked.

"'Everybody calls him Fitz-Mac, he's a well known writer and that's the name he signs. I don't know what his real name is. It's a question if he knows what it is himself, he don't hear it from anybody that knows him and everybody knows him.'

"Now, girls don't laugh at us and don't be scandalized, but somehow or other we got acquainted with Fitz-Mac, and a very nice gentleman he proved to be.

"There is much to interest one at Grand Junction, so named because it is situated at the confluence of the Gunnison with the Grand River and ———"

"Tell us more about Fitz-Mac"—interrupted Jennie.

"Hush, child," said Julia severely, "we're studying scenery."

"Not when there is an interesting man in the foreground," replied Jennie.

"Very well," said Judith, "I'll describe Fitz-Mac first, and Grand Junction afterward. The gentleman would be characterized by the novelist as 'still young.' He is of medium height, has dark eyes and hair and a full beard trimmed to a peak, a la Parisian. His smile, as Mrs. Gamp would say, is ''eavingly ' his voice soft, low and cultivated, his manner polished and debonaire."

"Ah!" sighed Jennie, "I wish I'd gone over the Rio Grande."

"Grand Junction," said Judith, "is a thriving town of 3,000 inhabitants, situated in the great fruit growing belt of

Colorado. Mining, agriculture and the raising of sheep and cattle also help to make for its prosperity. Here the Denver and Rio Grande connects with the Rio Grande Western Railway, the latter line extending from Grand Junction to Salt Lake City and Ogden, though there is no change of cars, the sleeper taken at Denver running through to San Francisco. Ten miles beyond Grand Junction we passed through the little town of Fruita, which is famous for the fact that around it are the finest fruit orchards in Colorado. Leaving Fruita the line passes on for eight miles through orchard lands and then we plunge once more into the depths of the Cañon of the Grand River. What can I say to convey to you the grandeur of the scene? The stupendous majesty of this rocky way rifted through the mountains is beyond the power of description. The glowing colors of the Ruby Amphitheater, the flaming splendor of Flamingo Rocks, the grotesque figures in everlasting stone of the 'Mulligan Guards' and the almost innumerable points of especial interest defy all my attempts at word painting. Beyond the cañon is the desert. Arid expanses of shifting sand, treeless, shrubless, verdureless, dead! But ready to blossom like the rose under the influence of irrigation. On the horizon to our left, distant fifty miles, rise the serrated summits of the LaSal mountains, while to the right we can see the castellated formations of the Book Cliffs.

"It was during our crossing of the desert that 'Fitz Mac' told us about the attractions of southern Colorado. 'This part of the State,' said he, 'can be reached by the Denver and Rio Grande Railroad and its extensions, known as the Rio Grande Southern and the Silverton Railroad. These lines have also various branches, so that every part of the mountain and valley region south of the Arkansas River is easily reached. The leading towns of the southwest are Alamosa, Montevista, Del Norte and Wagonwheel Gap in the San Luis Valley, and beyond Wagonwheel Gap, which is a great health resort, possessing wonderful hot springs, is Creede, the recently discovered and exceedingly rich silver camp. Durango is the metropolis of the Animas Valley,

Spearfish Falls, South Dakota, on Burlington Route

while Silverton, in Baker's Park, is the center of a great gold and silver mining region. The scenery of southern Colorado is grand and beautiful. Toltec Gorge, Animas Cañon, Wagonwheel Gap, Baker's Park, Red Mountain, Mount Abrams, are all worth a trip across the continent to see. The Denver and Rio Grande Railroad, recognizing this fact, have established special rates during the summer season for a journey from Denver to Silverton, thence over the range to Ouray, and back to Denver. This tour is called 'The Trip Around the Circle,' and embraces in its thousand miles more marvels of scenic interest than any other journey of a thousand miles in the world. The Rio Grande Southern Railroad extends from Durango to Rico, Telluride, and back to the main line at Ridgway. It is by this line that one reaches the mysterious ruins of the cliff dwellings, the dismantled homes of a race long since forgotten. These cliff houses are built of hewn stone laid in a cement that is harder than the stone itself. Who the mysterious people were, how long ago they lived and what was their fate, are questions that are yet unanswered. The towns of Rico and Telluride are thriving mining centers, and famous for their output of gold and silver ore. I could talk to you for hours about this wonderful country, but we are approaching Green River, and I will stop talking and suggest that we go out on the platform and take a look at the river and its surroundings.'

"Complying with our friend's request——"

"Oh, he's 'our friend,' is he?" interrupted Jennie.

"We all went out to the platform," continued Judith, ignoring the interruption though a flushed cheek signaled the fact that she felt the mischievious thrust, "and we were well paid for our trouble. The river is most appropriately named for its waters are deeply tinged with green. It is a peculiarity of the streams in the Rocky Mountains that they are individualized by marked differences in color. The waters of the Animas River are deeply blue; those of the Gunnison slightly yellow, the Eagle has a silvery tint while the Grand River is brown in hue. Though Green River Station is in the

CROW INDIAN AGENCY, SOUTH DAKOTA, ON BURLINGTON ROUTE.

desert its grounds are beautified with green sward, flowering shrubs and thrifty trees, all owing their existence to the magic of irrigation, and convincing the most skeptical that these barren, arid wastes can be reclaimed and made fertile through the influence of water. This is a dining station of the Rio Grande Western, and with that at Helper is famed among tourists for unusual excellence. Beyond Green River the desert extends a distance of sixty-four miles to the town of Price, which is situated on Price River, from which it is named. This desert, however, is being steadily reclaimed by the introduction of irrigating ditches and in course of time will become fertile farming and orchard lands. Leaving the Price River behind us we enter regions of more picturesque interest and soon behold the famed Castle Gate whose rock built bastions rise on either side of the track leaving but a narrow way for the train to enter. This is the gateway to the Wasatch range of mountains and the ascent is soon begun.

"Soldier Summit, which derives its name from the fact that a soldier of Albert Sidney Johnston's army died and was buried here, is the crest of the range over which the line passes at an altitude of 7,465 feet. For twenty miles we wind downward through romantic scenery on the western slope of the Wasatch and at Thistle we enter the shadows of Spanish Fork Cañon, a gorge in the mountains that abounds in most varied and striking views. I have been a spendthrift of words and have no language that can impart to you the grandeur and variety of this cañon. I can only say that every moment passed within its depths abounded in keen delight. At the western end of the gorge nestle Castilla Springs, one of the most famous health resorts of Utah. Here are a handsome brown stone hotel and many neat cottages for the accommodation of guests who seek these marvelous healing springs in search of health and recreation. The altitude of the springs is 4,920 feet and the distance from Ogden only ninety-eight miles. Sixteen miles beyond we pass through Provo, a typical Mormon town famous as a health resort and for its fruits and vegetables, and find ourselves traversing Utah Valley, with a charming view of Utah Lake, laying bright and beautiful, only three miles distant to the southward. From this lake the Jordan river, whose course we cross twice near Jordan Narrows, runs down to the Great Salt Lake. At Bingham Junction, one branch line strikes off to the rich Bingham mines sixteen miles southwest. Another branch, ten miles long, runs to Wasatch at the mouth of Little Cottonwood Cañon, where all the white granite for the Mormon temple in Salt Lake City was quarried. For four miles on both sides the cañon is walled with this beautiful stone. From Wasatch a tramway leads to Alta where the famous Emma mine is located. In quick succession we pass Brigham Junction, Germania and Francklyn, and reach the goal of our ambition, Salt Lake City.

CHAPTER V.

SALT LAKE CITY AND THE GREAT SALT SEA.

> "When the desert shall grow green,
> And when ships shall there be seen;
> When fresh water streams shall pour
> Into Salt Sea, evermore,
> And the Sea shall salter grow;
> Then the sons of men may know
> That the time is drawing near
> When the world shall disappear."
> —*Mother Shipton's Prophecy.*

MOTHER SHIPTON must have had a very clear vision of Salt Lake Valley and the Great Salt Lake when she wrote her famous prophecy," said Judith, as she read the lines which head this chapter, "but while her premises are correct, her conclusion is certainly false, for the world doesn't show the least signs of disappearing. I, for one, should be very sorry if it did, for the world is very attractive to me just now and especially this corner of it. Salt Lake City has a peculiar charm for me and I find here the survivals of a most peculiar and quaint civilization. The advent of the Gentiles and their accession to power are working a great change, and modern methods of business and architecture are fast transforming the appearance of the city. The patriarchal government of Brigham Young is now a thing of the past, but the Tabernacle, the Temple and Assembly Hall, together with the Lion House, the Amelia Palace, and other buildings of a like character remain as monuments of the days when Mormonism ruled this valley. Picturesque for situation, Salt Lake City, embowered in shade trees, with rivulets of water coursing down each side of her streets, with verdant lawns, blushing rose bushes, flowering shrubs in luxuriant profusion, surrounded by mountains and near the margin of the mysterious Salt Sea, commands our admiration and stands unique among the cities of the world. Every house in the city is surrounded by green lawns, gardens and orchards, so that one looks in vain for a poor man's home. The humblest adobe cottage, half hidden in trees, fruit and flowers, becomes a thing of beauty. In fact, the emblem of Mormonism was a

GRAVES OF SOLDIERS ON THE FIELD WHERE CUSTER FELL.

Bee Hive, and every man, woman and child had to work at something. Under Mormon rule everybody was a producer. No drones were tolerated, and there were no loafers, tramps or beggars. The whole city was abloom with industry and thrift.

"As to the present status of the city, Colonel Donan furnishes me with the following facts: Only within the last three or four years has the spirit of modern Gentile progress reached this quaintest, most beautiful and most interesting of

North American cities. Its population rose from 20,678 in 1880, to 46,259 in 1890, and it is now between 50,000 and 55,000. The assessed value of property sprang from $10,611,752 in 1889, to $54,353,740 in 1890; an increase of 227 per cent. in a single year. As the assessment is on a basis of one-fifth to one-fourth of actual valuation, the true value of real estate and personal property in the city is over $200,000,000; but put it at only double the assessor's figures and it amounts to $108,707,480, which, in a place of 50,000 population, is an average of more than $2,000 for every inhabitant within its municipal limits. This has no parallel in any other American city, if it has in the world.

"Temple Block is one of the first objects of curious interest that we visited. It is a square containing an area of ten acres surrounded by a wall fifteen feet high and five feet thick. In it stand the magnificent Mormon Temple, the Tabernacle and the Assembly Hall. The Temple is, with the single exception of St Patrick's Cathedral in New York, the grandest and costliest ecclesiastical structure in the country. It was begun in 1853, and is just completed at a cost of nearly $6,000,000. It is two hundred feet long, a hundred feet wide, and a hundred feet high, with four towers, one at each corner, two hundred and twenty feet in height. The walls are ten feet thick, and the massiveness and solidity of its construction insure its defiance to the ravages of time for ages to come. It is built wholly of snow-white granite from the Cottonwood Cañon; and standing on one of the loftiest points in the city, it can be seen for fifty miles up and down the valley.

" The Tabernacle, which is just west of the Temple in the same square, is one of the architectural puzzles of the world. It looks like a vast terrapin-back, or half of a prodigious eggshell cut in two lengthwise, and is built wholly of iron, glass and stone. It is two hundred and fifty feet long, a hundred and fifty feet wide, and a hundred feet high in the center of the roof, which is a single mighty arch, unsupported by pillar or post, and is said to have but one counterpart on the globe. The walls are twelve feet thick, and there are twenty huge

David Davis Arm Chair.   Burlington Route.

double doors for entrance and exit. The Tabernacle seats 13,462 people, and its acoustic properties are so marvelously perfect that a whisper or the dropping of a pin can be heard all over it. The organ is one of the largest and grandest toned in existence, and was built here of native woods, by Mormon workmen and artists, at a cost of $100,000. It is fifty-eight feet high, has fifty-seven stops, and contains two thousand six hundred and forty-eight pipes, some of them nearly as large as the chimneys of a Mississippi River steamboat. The choir consists of from two hundred to five hundred trained voices, and the music is glorious beyond description. Much of it is in minor keys, and a strain of plaintiveness mingles with all its majesty and power. All the seats are free, and tourists from all parts of the world are to be found among the vast multitude that assembles at every service.

"Assembly Hall is of white granite, of Gothic architecture, and has seats for 2,500. The ceiling is elaborately frescoed with scenes from Mormon history, including the delivery of the golden plates, containing the New Revelation to the Prophet Joseph Smith, by the Angel Moroni. The hall contains a superb organ of native woods and home workmanship.

"Salt Lake City is surrounded by lovely pleasure grounds and unsurpassable health resorts. The mountains and cañons afford an endlessly varied field for summer tourist recreation; and medicinal springs abound. The most famous of these are the Warm Springs, within the city limits, and the Hot Springs, about four miles out, both on electric street car lines. The water of Hot Springs has a temperature of 128°, and the flow is over 20,000 gallons an hour. It is noted for its curative power. The water of the Warm Springs, with a temperature of 103°, is piped into a superb natatorium in the heart of the city. The invalid here has the advantage of a climate that is as nearly perfect as can be found; dry, bracing, combining the salt air of the sea with the pure and rarified air of the mountains; where the sun shines nearly every day in the year; where there is no fog, miasma or malaria, and where

Horseshoe Curve, near Custer, South Dakota. Burlington Route.

the blizzards and sand storms that afflict other health resort regions are unknown."

"Doctor Judith, when do you propose to open an office?" asked Jennie, smiling at her friend's enthusiasm.

"Not now, and certainly not here. The climate is too strong a competitor," answered Judith.

"But Great Salt Lake has a fascination for me that cannot be shaken off. How can we account for this mysterious inland sea, 100 miles in length and an average of 25 miles in breadth; with an area of 2,500 square miles; with many fresh water tributaries and no known outlet; with an average depth of 20 feet, with an altitude of 4,250 feet above sea level, with waters six times as salt as those of the ocean, with four large rivers pouring into it and no perceptible rise of its surface and not the slightest diminution of its saline qualities?

"When, in February, 1846, twenty thousand Mormons, under the leadership of Brigham Young, started from Nauvoo, Illinois, on their two thousand mile pilgrimage through the trackless wilderness of the American West, they proclaimed themselves the modern Israel in search of the promised land. As Colonel Donan says: It was a strange fate, or destiny, or Providence, that led them to a region so similar to the 'Land of Promise' of Israel of old. There, the lake of Gennesaret, or sea of Galilee, was fresh water and full of fish. The Jordan River flowed out of it and emptied into the Dead Sea, which is so salt that no living thing is found in its waters. Here, Utah Lake is fresh and sweet, and its limpid waters swarm with speckled trout and other fish as savory as any that strained the nets of Peter, James and John. Out of it flows the Mormon River Jordan, and after rambling for forty or fifty miles through orchards and meadows, grain fields and gardens, pours its silvery tide into Great Salt Lake, the saltest body of water on the globe, surpassing even its Judean counterpart by one and a half per cent. In the Holy Land the Jordan flows from North to South, while the Utah Jordan flows from South to North. Mount Nebo stood like a giant sentinel overlooking the ancient 'land flowing with milk and honey,' and here Mount Nebo, lifting its crown of eternal snow twelve thousand feet heavenward, stands guard forever over a fairer Canaan than that which Moses viewed, but never entered.

"It may seem preposterous to talk of the finest sea bathing on earth a thousand miles from the ocean; but truth is no less truth because it appears absurd. The sea bathing in Great Salt Lake infinitely surpasses anything of the kind on either the Atlantic or Pacific coasts. The water contains many times more salt and much more soda, sulphur, magnesia, chlorine, bromine and potassium than any ocean water on the globe. It is powerful in medicinal virtues. The specific gravity is but a trifle less than that of the Holy Land Dead Sea, the actual figures with distilled water as a unit being, for the ocean 1.027, for Salt Lake 1.107, and for the Dead Sea 1.116. The human body will not and cannot sink in it. You can walk out in it where it is fifty feet deep, and your body will stick up out of it, like a fishing cork, from the shoulders upward. You can sit down in it perfectly secure where it is fathoms deep. Any one can float upon it at the first trial; there is nothing to do but lie down gently upon it and float.

"Saltair Beach is without doubt the finest salt water bathing resort in the world. The magnificent building erected for the convenience of bathers, owes its existence to the enterprise of the Rio Grande Western Railway. It was built at a cost of over $300,000 and extending fully a half a mile into the lake, contains 1,000 bath rooms, and is one of the most attractive resorts in this region of wonderful attractions.

"But in the words of Captain Corcoran 'Though I'm anything but clever, I could talk like that forever,' and as we have yet to hear how the other girls fared on their journey from Denver to Ogden, I will stop right here."

CHAPTER VI.

DENVER TO OGDEN BY THE OVERLAND ROUTE.

"Along my trail the eagles fly
But not so far nor fast as I ;
I climb to where the rivers rise,
Where mountains escalade the skies,
Where baby rivers, doubting rest,
To turn their footsteps East or West."

—*Song of the Locomotive.*

"WHILE Julia and Judith were speeding southward over the Denver and Rio Grande to Pueblo" began Jennie, "Joan and I were flying northward over the Union Pacific to Cheyenne."

"And yet we've met, though going in opposite directions," exclaimed Julia. "That proves the world is round."

"It would if both roads did'nt turn westward."

"In that case they're parallel and the fact that we're all here must prove that parallel lines can meet."

"Nonsense! It proves that both the Rio Grande Western and the Union Pacific reach Salt Lake city, and I suppose you want me to tell you how the Union Pacific does it?"

"Certainly."

"In that case I require nothing but silence from you and mighty little of that, as the Irishman said.

"From Denver the through trains for San Francisco go northward 106 miles to Cheyenne, Wyoming, which is the junction point of the two main stems of the Union Pacific, the Nebraska main line, 516 miles from Omaha, and the Kansas main line 746, via Denver, from Kansas City.

Town Hot Springs. Hotel.

We enjoyed the run from Denver to Cheyenne very highly, at least *I* did, because it gave me an opportunity to traverse the oldest in point of settlement and most highly cultivated agricultural region of Colorado. Of course this wasn't so much of a novelty to Joan as she is a Colorado girl. For a part of the way we followed down to the Platte River and beheld as beautiful fields of grass and grain as one could find anywhere.

"The town of Greeley attracted my attention because it is the pioneer settlement, and here was first demonstrated the magic of irrigation in the State. Greeley is a clean, handsome town of 2,500 people, perfectly shaded by trees, and one of the most beautiful cities in Colorado. Besides being situated in the midst of a garden spot, its citizens have taken great pains to set out shade trees on their grounds and along the sidewalks, lay out lawns, and plant flowers, shrubbery, and vines about their houses. An excellent system of waterworks, with ample supply of water, affords all an opportunity to keep the lawns and gardens well watered, and the result is almost an annual transformation in the appearance of the city. In fact, more than half of the town is hidden in foliage. To our left we had the Snowy Range constantly in view, with Long's tremendous peak standing sentry at the northern extremity.

"Cheyenne, 6,050 feet in altitude, with a population of 12,744 is one of the sprightliest and most prosperous of cities in the entire West. It is well and compactly built, and for many years has been the center of the cattle industry of the Northwest. It constituted for a long time the outpost of civilization, becoming embodied in the legends of border life, and is a place of rare historical interest. Cheyenne possesses all the modern improvements—gas, electric light, street car service and most of the luxuries of city life. From Cheyenne a branch of the Union Pacific runs north through a magnificent agricultural country to Douglas, Wyoming, 167 miles distant.

"Sherman, a small station just west of Cheyenne, at an

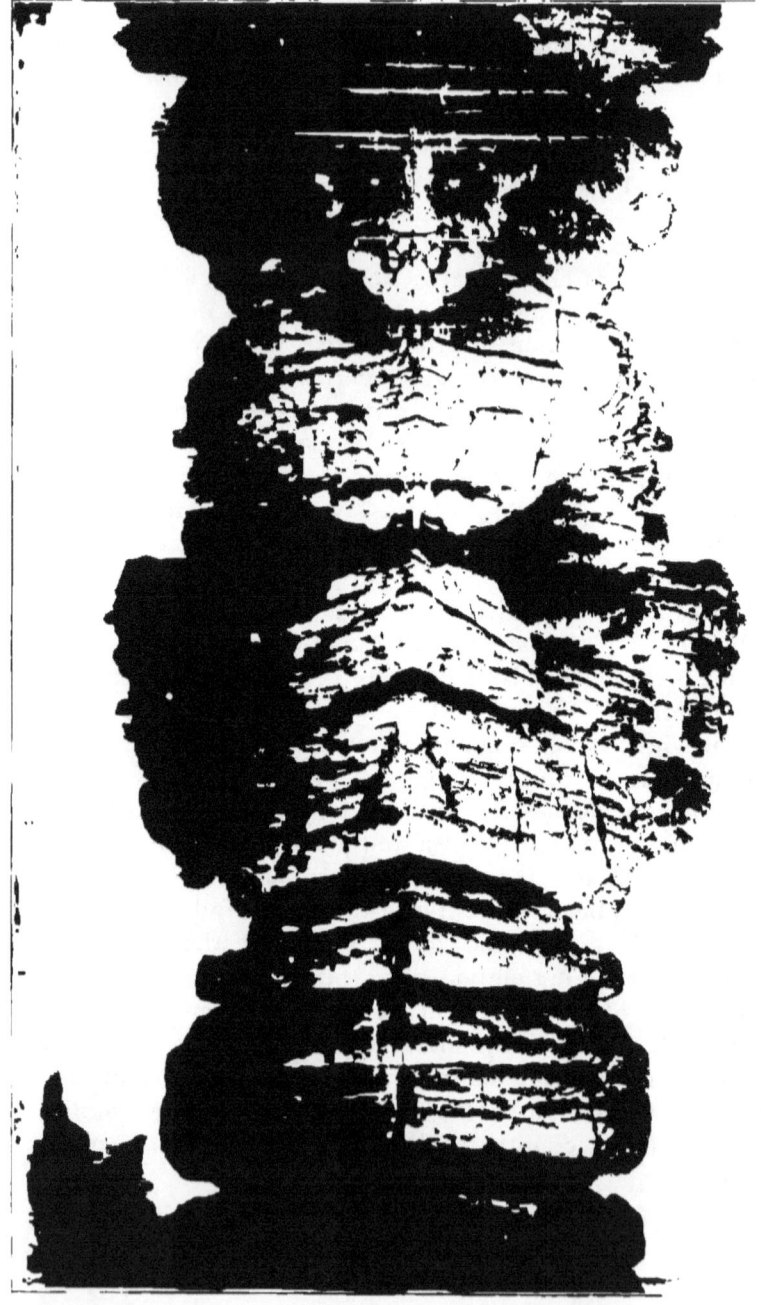

Sylvan Lake, near Custer, South Dakota. Burlington Route

elevation of 8,247 feet, is the loftiest point in the transcontinental ride. From Sherman can be seen Long's peak, nearly 200 miles away. Near the station is the Ames Monument, a pyramidal granite structure sixty-five feet in height, with a base sixty feet square, which was erected by the Union Pacific Railway to the memory of the Ames Brothers, to whom the completion of the Union Pacific was largely due. The scenery is wild and rugged. Just beyond Sherman is Dale Creek bridge, one of the most remarkable sights of the overland trip. The structure is of iron and stretches from bluff to bluff with a 650-foot span. The train passes over it just 127 feet above the creek, which looks like a mere rivulet below. Pike's peak can be seen away off to the south, not less than 165 miles distant.

"Laramie has an elevation of 7,149 feet above sea level, and a population of 6,388. It is one of the principal towns on the main line of the Union Pacific between Council Bluffs and Ogden. Then come Rawlins, Rock Springs and Green River, where the trains for Portland, Oregon, are made up, although they do not take their departure from the main line until Granger is reached, thirty miles west of Green River, and the trip across the continent is continued to the great Northwest. The road goes along over moderate curves and grades, through pretty little valleys along the Bear River, until the great territory of Idaho is entered at Border Station. Then on through Soda Springs and Pocatello—the junction with the Utah and Northern branch for Butte, Garrison and Helena. Next, Shoshone Station is reached, where the junction is made for the Great Shoshone Falls, via stage, and also for Hailey and Ketchum, via rail; thence from Shoshone Station the road stretches away through Nampa, where the junction is made with the Idaho Central branch for Boise City, nineteen miles distant; and on the train goes from Nampa, through Caldwell and Weiser to Huntington, within Oregon; thence from Huntington through Baker City, Union, La Grande, Pendleton and Umatilla Junction to 'The Dalles,' which takes its name from the dalles of the Columbia. From this point on to East Portland the trip is one replete with scenic wonders. Arriving in Portland, which is the metropolis of the Northwest Pacific coast, and a large, handsome cosmopolitan city, the trip 'Across the Continent' to Portland, Oregon, is complete.

"There are many objects of interest in and around Green River, among which are the peculiar clay buttes by which it is surrounded. From Green River the trip across the continent is continued. At Wasatch Station the summit of the Wasatch range of mountains is reached. The elevation is 6,824 feet, and at this point the road enters Echo Cañon. Echo Creek, which runs through the cañon, is crossed thirty-one times in twenty-six miles. Three and a half miles west of Wasatch, the train runs into a tunnel 900 feet long. At Echo Station, Weber Cañon is entered. One and a half miles west of Echo can be seen the 'Witch Rocks.' Five miles further on is the 1,000 mile tree, which is just 1,000 miles from Omaha, and a mile further on is the 'Devil's Slide.' Echo and Weber cañons compare favorably with the celebrated Colorado cañons. Three and a half miles west of Corydon, the cañon broadens out, and to the left are noticed the first of the Mormon settlements. About one-half way between Peterson and Uintah Station, 'Devil's Gate' is to be seen, and shortly after, the country widens into the Great Salt Lake Valley, when Ogden is reached. The first view of the valley after the surfeit of mountain scenery, is one of striking contrast, quiet and pleasant to the eye. Ogden is 1,034 miles from Council Bluffs, and 833 miles from San Francisco.

"Ogden is pushing, prosperous and picturesque. It occupies a strong point of vantage at the junction of the Weber and Ogden Rivers and is possessed of magnificent water power. On a bench of Great Salt Lake it overlooks that inland sea, and has a wide horizoned view of mountain and valley. Its population is above the 20,000 mark and its growth rapid and secure. The whole surrounding country is rich in mines of gold, silver, copper, lead and iron, and the

The Entrance to Wind Cave, Hot Springs, South Dakota — Burlington Route

bonanzas of LaPlata are almost at the doors of Ogden. The famous Utah Hot Springs, where many marvelous cures have been effected, are near the city, and a charming bathing resort on the Salt Lake beach is in plain view of the courthouse. The ride from Ogden to Salt Lake City is full of interest. We rushed for eighteen miles, through fields waving with growing grain and orchards bending under their burdens of bloom, through Hooper and Layton, and Kaysville where two Mormon farmers recently raised a hundred and six bushels of wheat to the acre and sold it, measuring that number of bushels for every acre they had in cultivation, to the great Zion store in Salt Lake City. On we go four miles further to Farmington, where a spur of track runs down to the Lake Park Bathing Beach with its pavilions and piers, bath houses, verandas and promenades, and its extensive salt works ; on past Lake Shore Station, where tens of thousands of tons of salt are made without cost from the wondrous lake waters ; past Wood's Crossing and Hot Springs, where a flood of almost boiling water pours from the side of a granite cliff, as full of healing virtues as those of Arkansas or Carlsbad or Baden Baden ; on amid meadows of sweet scented alfalfa and orchards of peaches and apricots, nectarines, apples and plums, with the grand Wasatch peaks always on the left hand and the azure expanse of the great lake on the right. 'Whoop !' goes the whistle and looking out of the window we see the spires of the Temple and the next minute, the train stops at the station and we are in Salt Lake City and the arms of Judith and Julia."

"A regular Lady Gay Spanker speech," said Judith.

"You don't lack in London Assurance," answered Jennie. "Now let's go to dinner."

CHAPTER VII.

ONWARD TO THE GOLDEN GATE—THEN HOMEWARD.

> "Westward!" the Chieftains cry,
> "Westward!" the braves reply ;
> "Westward to where our fortunes wait
> Beside the Golden Gate."
> <div style="text-align:right">—<i>The Braves Foray.</i></div>

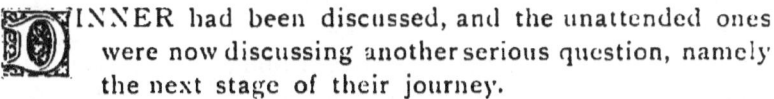INNER had been discussed, and the unattended ones were now discussing another serious question, namely the next stage of their journey.

"We really must move on," said Joan.

"Don't say move on," remarked Jennie, "you're not a policeman."

"No, but we must move on just the same."

"We don't need a committee on ways and means," said Judith, "because in the matter of 'means,' we've our tickets, and as to 'ways,' there's only one way and that's over the Central Pacific Railroad."

"Southern Pacific, you mean, dear," corrected Julia.

"Everything must be southern with you," replied Judith. "I suppose you're correct, but everybody calls the line from Ogden to San Francisco the Central Pacific, and one might as well be dead as out of the fashion, and I'd call it the Central Pacific if its real name were the Circumference Pacific, so there!"

The following day saw the four young ladies comfortably ensconced in a section of the San Francisco Pullman in a position for the first time since the beginning of their journey to indulge in whist without a dummy and to buy four apples for a dime and all be present to dispose properly of them.

The journey was made in this happy quartette fashion until Sacramento was reached, at which point Judith and Joan took the Southern Pacific branch to Los Angeles, and Jennie and Julia continued onward to San Francisco, with the understanding that they should journey southward from that city to Pasadena and join the others at the Hotel Raymond.

Perhaps the best way to give an idea of that portion of the journey which the young ladies made in company will be to quote some extracts from a letter Judith wrote to her father in which she said: "From Ogden the trip is made on the Central Pacific Railroad, over great plains and through immense snow sheds, great mountain ranges, beautiful valleys and jagged foothills.

"Leaving Ogden, the train passes Promontory, which was intended to be the point of junction of the two roads forming the transcontinental route, namely, the Union and Central Pacific Railroads. Later on, Ogden was decided upon as a compromise.

"The crowning scenes of the trip across Utah, Nevada, and California are not reached until Reno is passed. Cape Horn, Emigrant Gap, the Sierra Nevadas, Donner Lake, and other objects of more than ordinary interest then attracted our attention.

"Nevada, of course, is celebrated for her famous mines. The great mines of Virginia City and the Sutro Tunnel attract numerous visitors. The marvelous Carson and Humboldt sinks, in which the waters of all the rivers in the State of Nevada, save one, are swallowed, the Mud Lakes, the Borax marshes, and countless numbers of thermal springs, have been the wonder of the scientist and the delight of the tourist. One hundred and fifty-five miles from Reno is Sacramento, a beautiful city and the capital of California. It is delightfully located upon the east bank of the Sacramento river, in the midst of the most productive grain fields, vine-

Teepee, or Devil's Tower, Wyo.   Burlington Route

yards and orchards in the world. The climate is delightful and the surrounding country entrancing."

It must be confessed that this was a very brief summary of the attractions of the journey from Ogden to Sacramento, but it should be understood that Judith was busy looking at the marvelous scenery, and did'nt have much time to write out her impressions. But when the party met at the Raymond a few days after separating at Sacramento, the flow of conversation made ample amends for the lack in the flow of ink.

"Judith and I have been having a lovely time at the Raymond," said Joan to Julia and Jennie, as the four friends gathered for a "good talk" in a quiet corner of the hotel piazza.

"This is the most lovely hotel, in the loveliest spot of the loveliest country, with the loveliest climate in the whole world," exclaimed Judith enthusiastically.

"And it's full of the loveliest people," began Joan.

"Including ourselves," concluded Julia.

"Isn't this a vision of beauty?" cried Jennie, pointing to the landscape spread out beneath them. "How restful to the eye and mind of the tired traveler, that broad expanse of vineyards, while the hills and vales of Pasadena glowing with the rich green foliage of the orange and lemon trees, amid which we can see stately villas and picturesque cottages, add to the variety and picturesqueness of the scene."

"And yonder are the mountains," exclaimed Julia, pointing to the northward.

"Yes," said Joan with the air of an old resident, "Those nearer us are the Sierra San Fernando, while the further range, etherially blue against the sky, is the lofty wall of the Sierra Madre."

"There is only one fault I find with the management of the Raymond," said Judith, "and that is that they do not keep the hotel open the entire year. It is such a marvel of excellence that it seems a shame to have it silent and almost deserted for any part of the year. You know it is owned by

Mr. Walter Raymond, of Boston, Mass , one of the firm of Raymond and Whitcomb, the great excursion managers. By the way, the hotel Colorado, at Glenwood Springs, Colo., is also owned by Mr. Raymond."

"The building is certainly magnificent in its proportions and it occupies one of the grandest of situations," said Jennie.

"And I can assure you that its accommodations are fully up to the highest standard of excellence," remarked Joan.

"It is certainly a most charming place," said Julia.

"Oh! you don't know half the charm of the Raymond yet. We have made new discoveries each day," exclaimed Judith. "Every improvement that modern hotel science could suggest, or money supply, has been introduced. The spacious grounds—fifty-five acres, think of that, exhibit the handsomest and most elaborate results possible in the way of landscape gardening. There are ornamental fountains, rose, palm, and cactus gardens, tennis courts, children's playgrounds, croquet grounds, swings, bowling alleys, beneath an arbor of trailing vines, and other features. There are also a large orange grove and a sloping lawn diversified with flowers and shrubs. Among the trees which adorn the long slopes are the pepper, eucalyptus, or Australian gum, pine. cypress, sycamore, giant redwood, olive, date, palm, banana. pomegranate, guava, Japanese persimmon, umbrella, maple. elm, locust, English walnut, birch, ailantus, poplar, willow, and a great variety of ornamental shrubs. Several greenhouses and a nursery on one side of the hill are stocked with many thousands of the rarest and most beautiful plants."

"You spoke about the umbrella tree," said Jennie. " Pray what kind of a tree is that?"

"The umbrella tree," said Joan learnedly, "is a native of Japan (*Melia Speciosa*). It has a straight, slender trunk, with compact foliage of dark green leaves, resembling somewhat those of the ash. No tree makes a denser shade. It is a fairly quick grower, making a crown more than a rod across when seven years old. In spring it is literally covered with small lilac flowers which emit a delicate perfume."

"Think of an umbrella emitting a delicate perfume!" said Jennie.

"Or with a crown more than a rod across," added Julia.*

"But tell us about your trip to San Francisco," remarked Joan.

"It can't be told," replied Jennie, "the trip from Sacramento to San Francisco is a revelation. I felt like Alice in Wonderland, everything was new and strange and lovely, and when San Francisco was reached I was in such a state of delight that I had no words to express my feelings. San Francisco is the Paris of America. It is full of life and light and beauty. Golden Gate Park, Sutro Park, the magnificent bay, the Golden Gate, the great ocean, seal rocks, and hundreds of points of interest claimed our attention and aroused our enthusiasm. I tell you, girls, we've made a mistake. We should have planned a six months' stay in California and I for one will never be satisfied until I realize that experience."

For six perfect days the young ladies lingered at the Raymond. Each day filled with excursions to the many points of interest which abound in the vicinity of Pasadena and Los Angeles, then they bade that delightful region a regretful farewell and turned their faces northward on their homeward journey. In order to enjoy new experiences the return was made by the way of the Central and Northern Pacific lines to Billings, Montana, from which point the Burlington route extends to Omaha and Chicago.

Montana although one of the newest of lands so far as the advance of modern life is concerned, is yet historic, for on its ground made sacred by heroic sacrifice, fell brave Custer and his men. Only two hours and a half ride from

---

*Since the above was written the Raymond has been entirely destroyed by fire, but the owner has perfected plans for its rebuilding on a grander and more perfect scale of magnificence than ever. The hotel will be completed and ready for use by the opening of the next excursion season.—*Editor*.

A California Reminiscence.

Billings, brought the young ladies to the Crow Agency and the scene of Custer's fight and fall. The party broke their journey here for one day to do honor to the memory of the great Custer, by visiting the scene of his tragic death. In 1876 befell the sad event which shall never pass from the memory of man. In the words of Professor Wheeler " Here it was that Custer fell into that fatal trap, and here it was that Rain-in-the-Face wreaked his revenge on the invader of his rocky refuge :

<blockquote>
" In that desolate land and lone
Where rolls the Yellowstone."
</blockquote>

"Here feats of valor were performed that deserve to be chronicled with those of Leonidas at Thermopylæ but which met with a more tragic and awful reward. On the banks of the Rosebud death lurked, and no strength of will, no desperate courage, no wiliest strategy could defeat him.

"The history of that awful day is written in blood, and the memory of the heroism that was there displayed, shall never pass away from earth.

" At the northern end of a rather prominent ridge a slight knoll rises and we can discern that there is even something more than this. It is the Custer monument, planted on the most commanding point of the ridge, and at the spot where Custer and most of his officers and men went down. There Custer himself, Yates, Smith, Tom Custer, Cook, and others fell together.

" The battlefield is now a national cemetery, and at different spots in it interments have been made of soldiers who were killed in the Northwest in other Indian fights. Many bodies originally interred at old Fort Phil Kearney, Wyoming, Fort C. F. Smith and Fort Shaw, Montana, have been reinterred here.

"Since the battle this country has been given to the Crow Indians, and a fine reservation it makes. Within a couple of miles of the battle monument is located the agency, which makes quite a settlement. The two most conspicuous objects are the flagstaff, with the stars and stripes flying, and

PLUNGE BATH, HOT SPRINGS, SOUTH DAKOTA.

a fine brick schoolhouse. Besides the agent and his clerical force, there are also a number of teachers, a physician, and the usual necessary employes. A tavern, two or three stores and several dwelling houses are also found. Indian police are constantly on duty, but find little of a disagreeable nature to keep them employed."

Resuming their journey with feelings tinged with sadness, but soon rising with the buoyancy of youth, the unattended ones were on the *qui vive* to behold the novel scenes of this strange new land. On entering Wyoming their attention was called by the Pullman conductor to the fact that there were now passing through one of the richest agricultural regions of the Great West. "Sheridan County," said he "is now attracting wide attention, its resources being truly wonderful. The county is 100 miles long by thirty wide, and has an area of 3,000 square miles. It has 1,980,000 acres, of which 640,000 are agricultural, 960,000 grazing and 380,000 timber and mountain country."

In order to secure one more experience of the delights of mountain health resorts, the party made a side trip over a branch of the Burlington Route to the Hot Springs, of South Dakota. Standing at the threshold of the Black Hills, there could be no more favorable location for a summer and winter resort than Hot Springs. Embosomed as it is within the Hills, picturesquely placed upon Fall river, with an altitude of 3,500 feet (2,500 feet higher than Chicago), the atmosphere is at once clear, pure and dry, absolutely free from malaria, and the miasmatic vapors which now and then spread over less elevated places. The air, freighted with the scent of the great pine and spruce forests that are the crowning beauty of the Hills, giving them a kaleidoscopic charm that is possessed by no other portion of the Northwest, appeals strangely to the men and women who, in this work-a-day world, need just such a tonic as found at Hot Springs. When the dog star rules the world, when all is hot and muggy and life seems a pall, thousands of favored mortals in need of the medicinal qualities of the springs or sweet, pleasant rest, turn their steps toward this new resort in the Black Hills, and meet there the delight of living.

Over Mammoth Spring, but a short distance from the principal hotels, in the north part of the city, a magnificent plunge bath, 50 x 250 feet, has been built of stone, iron and wood, and provided with all the conveniences and apparatus of the most famous natatoriums in the world. The water in this colossal bath tub, which contains 300,000 gallons, and varies in depth from four to eight feet, is never still, as it rushes out through an orifice at the south end of the building at the rate of 100,000 gallons per hour.

As to bath houses, Hot Springs finds itself splendidly equipped. First in importance is the new house recently built by the management of the Hotel Evans, and adjoining the "Palace Resort Hotel of the West," by a covered passageway. It is of pink sandstone, three stories in height and conforms in architecture to the hotel, of which it is a part. It is equipped with the most modern appliances for administering spray, electric, vapor, salt, needle and tub baths, and is in charge of a medical director of established reputation. In addition, there are magnificent Turkish and Russian baths for ladies and gentlemen, the water being supplied through pipes from the Minnekahta Spring only a hundred yards or so away. There are also the Stewart bath house, the Hot Springs House and Sanitarium baths and the bath house in connection with the Catholicon Hotel.

The hotels of Hot Springs are many and excellent. The young ladies were guests at the Evans, which leads in point of beauty, spaciousness and cuisine, is a mammoth five-story structure of pink sandstone, architecturally perfect in that all the rooms are "outside" rooms. It is capable of accommodating 300 guests. The Gillespie, immediately opposite the Evans, across Fall River, is second in size and importance, having accommodations for 125 persons. The Hot Springs House has good accommodations for seventy guests. In addition to these there are the Parrott, Davis, Avenue, Ferguson, Dudley and Catholicon.

After resting two days at the Hot Springs the young ladies resumed their journey.

"Now," said Judith, "We are really homeward bound, no more stops until Omaha is reached and then we will have to say good by."

All too soon they realized that their trip was nearing its end and yet when the porter announced "Omaha! change cars for Lincoln, Denver, Kansas City and St. Louis." the girls were in a flutter of excitement. Tears were in evidence, kisses were exchanged. They all disembarked, although Judith was going through to Chicago on the Burlington, and standing in a group on the depot platform continued their lengthened farewell.

"Well, good-by, dears," exclaimed Judith.

"Good-by, you old darling," replied the rest in chorus.

"Good-by, Joan."

"Good-by, Judith."

"Be sure to write."

"Yes, I will, good-by Jennie."

"Good-by Julia."

"You'll all come to see me in September?"

"Yes, sure, good-by Jennie."

"And next year we'll take this unattended journey all over again?"

"Indeed we will. Good-by."

"Good-by."

"Wait a minute. When we go again we'll stay a month in Denver."

"Yes, and a month in Colorado Springs."

"Yes, and two months in Manitou."

"Right you are, and two months in Glenwood Springs."

"Yes, and two months at Salt Lake."

"Sure, and a month in San Francisco."

"Certainly, and a month in Pasadena."

"Of course, and a month in Hot Springs."

"Won't that be jolly? and a month"

"Hold on, girls!" said Judith, "If you stop a month longer any where you'll have used up the whole year and left no time to go and come in. Good gracious! my train's moving. I *must* go. Good-by."

"Good-by!"

"Good-by!"

"Good-by!"

INDEX TO ILLUSTRATIONS.

A Typical Chicago Street	Frontispiece
An Elkhorn Monument. Estes Park, Colorado, 60 miles from Denver. Burlington Route	7
Fall River, Estes Park, Colorado. Burlington Route	11
Teton Range from the East. Burlington Route	12
Among the Foot-Hills, Estes Park, Colorado. Burlington Route	13
Estes Cone, Estes Park, Colorado. Burlington Route	14
Devil's Slide. Union Pacific System, near Ogden	15
Tunnel No. 3. Weber Cañon, Utah. On Union Pacific System	16
Bluffs of Green River. Union Pacific System	17
From the Union Depot up Seventeenth Street, Denver Colo. Population 175,000. Altitude 5,285 feet	18
Cathedral Spires. Garden of the Gods, near Manitou, Colo	19
Gateway Garden of the Gods. D. & R. G. R. R., Looking West. Pike's Peak in the Distance	20
Balanced Rock, Garden of the Gods, Manitou, Colo	21
The Grave of H. H., Cheyenne Mountain, 7 miles from Colorado Springs	22
Manitou Springs, Colo., 80 miles from Denver, via Denver & Rio Grande R. R. Elevation 6,324 feet	23
Cog Railroad up Pike's Peak, Manitou, Colo	24
Pike's Peak, Cog Wheel R. R. Timber Line	25
Mother Judy, Monument Park, 9 miles from Colorado Springs, Colo	26
Summit of Pike's Peak, 88 miles from Denver. Elevation 14,714 feet	27
Pike's Peak Avenue, Colorado Springs, Colo. On Denver & Rio Grande R. R. Antler's Hotel at Base of Pike's Peak	28
High Bridge of the Loop above Georgetown, Colo. Union Pacific, Denver & Gulf R. R.	29
Amphitheater, Williams Cañon, Manitou, Colo	30
The Loop. Union Pacific, Denver & Gulf R. R., near Silver Plume, Colo	31
Ute Pass, Manitou, Colo. The Old Indian Trail to the Springs	32
Green Lake, above Georgetown, Colo. Union Pacific, Denver & Gulf R. R., near the Loop	32
The Snowy Range from the Arkansas Valley near Buena Vista. Denver, Leadville & Gunnison R. R.	33
Railroad Cut Thrown Out with One Blast. On the Florence & Cripple Creek R. R.	34
Entrance to Cripple Creek Cañon. On the Florence & Cripple Creek R. R.	35
Sail Ship Rocks, Platte Cañon, near Denver. On the Denver, Leadville & Gunnison R. R.	36
Gold Miner's Cabin, Cripple Creek, Colo	37
Rotunda of Mineral Palace, Pueblo, Colo. The Palace was Erected at a Cost of $250,000, and Contains a Magnificent Mineral Exhibit	38
"Old King Cole;" Statue made of Colorado Coal, and Placed in the Mineral Palace, Pueblo, Colo	39
Trout Fishing, Wagon Wheel Gap, Colo	41
Wagon Wheel Gap, Colo. On Denver & Rio Grande R. R. Elevation 8,449 feet. Distance from Denver 311 miles. Health and Pleasure Resort. Hot Springs of Great Medicinal Qualities	41
Toltec Gorge. Denver & Rio Grande R. R., near Alamosa, Colo. Train is Shown Entering Tunnel near Summit of Peak at Right. Height of Walls, 1,800 feet	43
Phantom Curve. Denver & Rio Grande Railroad, near Alamosa, Colo	45
Cañon of the Rio Las Animas. D. & R. G. R. R. Silverton Branch. The Animas River is Shown Flowing between Walls 1,500 feet high	46
Needle Mountains from Animas Cañon. Distance from Denver 483 miles	47
Uneva Lake, Colo. On Denver, Leadville & Gunnison R. R.	49
Mt. Abrams on Toll Road Irontown to Ouray	50
Ouray, Colo., Gold and Silver Mining Town. Elevation 7,721 feet. Distance from Denver 389 miles	50
Lake San Cristoval, near Lake City, Colo	51
The Tree in the Rock. Florence & Cripple Creek R. R.	52
"Big Bend," on the Ouray and Silverton Toll Road. This Wagon Road was made through Mountains at an Expense of $100,000 a mile, where Difficult Rock Work was Done	53
Sultan Mountain and Baker's Park, with Silverton in the Distance. Elevation 9,221 feet. Distance from Denver, 495 miles. Population 2,500	55
Cliff Dweller's Home, Mesa Verde. Rio Grande Southern R. R.	56
Cliff Palace, Mesa Verde. Rio Grande Southern R. R.	57
Burro Train Transporting Timbers for the Mines, Silverton, Colo	58

Ophir Loop. Rio Grande Southern R. R.	59
The Royal Gorge. Grand Cañon of the Arkansas. On the Denver & Rio Grande R. R. Height of Walls, 2,627 feet. The Climax of Awful Grandeur. Length 7 miles. Distance from Denver 163 miles	60
Upper Twin Lakes, near Leadville, Colo. Denver & Rio Grande R. R.	61
Entrance to Brown's Palace	62
Curricante Needle. Black Cañon of the Gunnison. On Denver & Rio Grande R. R. Height of Walls, 2,500 feet. Length of Cañon, 14 miles. Distance from Denver 350 miles	64
Marshall Pass, Mount Ouray in the Distance. Elevation 10,856 feet. Distance from Denver 224 miles. Length of Pass, 36 miles	65
Monte Cristo Hotel, Salida, Colo.	66
Eagle River Cañon. Through Line Rio Grande R. R. Near Red Cliff. Mines and Tramways for Transporting Ore Shown in the Engraving. Distance from Denver 300 miles	67
Mount of the Holy Cross. Near Leadville. On the Denver & Rio Grande R. R.	68
Walls of the Cañon of Grand River. Denver & Rio Grande R. R.	69
Rounding the Curve. Cañon of Grand River. Denver & Rio Grande R. R.	70
Second Tunnel, Cañon of the Grand River. Denver & Rio Grande R. R.	71
Hotel Colorado and Bath House, Glenwood Springs, Colo. Health and Pleasure Resort. Hotel and Bathing Pool and Pavilion Erected at a Cost of over Half a Million Dollars	73
Castle Gate. Rio Grande Western R. R.	74
Long Bridge over the Grand River, at Grand Junction, Colo. Rio Grande Western R. R.	77
Provo Falls, Utah. Rio Grande Western R. R.	78
Cañon of Grand River. Rio Grande Western R. R.	80
Lookout Rocks, Cañon of Grand River. Rio Grande Western R. R.	81
Half Tunnel, Cañon of the Grand River. Rio Grande Western.	82
Temple Block, Salt Lake City, showing Mormon Temple, the Great Tabernacle and Assembly Hall	84
The Knutsford Hotel, Salt Lake City, Utah.	85
Saltair, South Front of Pavilion, The Noted Bathing Resort, Salt Lake. Rio Grande Western R. R.	86
American Natural Gas and Oil Co.'s Wells. Output 12,000,000 cubic feet daily. Great Salt Lake, Utah	87
Garfield Beach and Great Salt Lake, Utah, from the Cave. On Union Pacific System	88
Castilla Springs Health Resort, Spanish Fork Cañon. Rio Grande Western R. R.	88
Main Street, Ogden, Utah. On Union Pacific System	89
Liberty Cap. Mammoth Hot Springs. Yellowstone Park reached via Union Pacific System	91
Ames Monument, Sherman, Wyo. On the Union Pacific System	92
Giant's Tea Kettle, Green River, Wyo. On Union Pacific System	93
Witches Rock, Weber Cañon, Utah. On Union Pacific.	94
The Star Geyser, Yellowstone National Park, Wyo. Union Pacific System	96
Green River, Buttes, Wyo. Union Pacific System	97
Yellowstone Cañon. Yellowstone National Park. Reached via Union Pacific System	98
Pulpit Terraces, Mammoth Hot Springs, Yellowstone National Park. Reached via Union Pacific System	99
Great Shoshone Falls, Idaho. Reached via Union Pacific System	100
Great Shoshone Falls, Idaho, Looking down the Cañon. Reached via Union Pacific System	101
Castle Crags. Southern Pacific R. R.	102
El Capitan, Yosemite Valley, Cal. Reached via the Southern Pacific R. R.	103
Umbrella Tree, Pasadena, Cal.	104
Date Palm, Pasadena, Cal.	105
Market Street, San Francisco, Cal.	107
The Prize Tallyho, The Raymond, Pasadena, Cal.	108
The Raymond, Pasadena, Cal.	109
Magnolia Avenue, Riverside, Cal.	110
Midway Point, Cypress Drive, Monteroy, Cal.	113
Mt. Shasta, California, Altitude 14,440 feet. Reached via Shasta Route. Southern Pacific R. R.	116
Spearfish Cañon. On the Burlington Route	118
Spearfish Falls, South Dakota. On Burlington Route	121
Crow Indian Agency, South Dakota. On Burlington Route	123
Graves of Soldiers on the Field where Custer Fell	126
David Davis Arm Chair. Burlington Route	128
Horseshoe Curve, near Custer, South Dakota. Burlington Route.	130
Town Hot Springs. Hotel	134
Sylvan Lake, near Custer, South Dakota. Burlington Route	136
The Entrance to Wind Cave, Hot Springs, South Dakota. Burlington Route	139
Teepee, or Devil's Tower, Wyo. Burlington Route.	143
A California Reminiscence	147
Plunge Bath, Hot Springs, South Dakota	149

The ANTLERS
...Colorado Springs, Colo...

COLORADO SPRINGS stands easily at the head of the resort cities of the Rocky Mountain region. In the extent, variety and magnificence of the scenery by which it is environed, it is without a rival on the American continent and probably upon the globe; while its superb climate, which has made it the Mecca of health-seekers from every part of Christendom, lends an additional charm to the pleasure and satisfaction with which these wonders of scenery are viewed by the tourist. To fully enumerate these, much less to describe them, however briefly, is impossible here; it must suffice to say that in the immediate vicinity of Colorado Springs and within walking or driving distance are such world-famous scenic wonders as the Garden of the Gods, Glen Eyrie, Monument Park, Manitou Springs and Ute Pass; together with that king of stupendous and awe-inspiring cañons and the Rocky Mountain region's chief of all is great Pike's Peak, whose snowy summit may be gained either upon ponies by one of the several trails, by a four-in-hand over a finely constructed carriage or in the famous cog-wheel railroad.

THE ANTLERS, Colorado Springs' foremost hotel, occupies a commanding position upon the western edge of the city and in full view west of the great mountain range dominated by Pike's Peak. It is an imposing and strikingly handsome structure of some four or five stories in height and containing two hundred guest rooms. It is supplied with every appliance known to modern hotel construction, including the highest grade of cuisine and is conducted with a generous appreciation of the requirements of the class of travel it has during the past ten years secured in ever-increasing volume from all parts of the world who annually visit Colorado Springs. Its appointments are elegant throughout and in perfect taste, and its cuisine and service are held justly to rank with the foremost hotels of the land, matching its superb setting in forming a key to the supreme attractiveness of the Pike's Peak region in the mind of a world's clientele.

For all information, address

E. BARNETT,
THE ANTLERS, COLORADO SPRINGS, COLO.

INTERIOR OF H. H. TAMMEN'S MAIN SALES ROOM (Floor Space, 3,225 Feet).

 # H. H. TAMMEN

DENVER COLO...

TO ALL READERS of this I extend an invitation to visit my establishment.

I HAVE A LARGE, elegantly furnished museum, as the illustration of the interior of my salesroom shows.

YOU ARE INVITED to spend all day, an hour, or everyday, and no one will even ask you to make a purchase.

YOU WILL SEE gold ores, silver ores, copper, iron and many others in the various forms as they are dug up in the Rocky Mountains; crude and made into odd novelties.

OPALS, RUBIES, Garnet, and a world of beautiful gem stones, ready to be set in jewelry and all mounted up.

INDIAN RELICS; not only the ancient things found in the ruins of the cliff dwellers, but blankets, beaded work and curios, pottery, made by the Indian of to-day.

A DISPLAY OF AGATES, in the rough and polished, made into all sort of things—button hooks, charms, chains, hat pins, etc.

ELK, LION, DEER, antelope and buffalo heads—yes, 200 of them decorate my walls.

THERE ARE 10,000 DIFFERENT THINGS I'm glad to show you. If you don't visit me send a stamp for my great illustrated catalog. Be sure and always remember the name.

H. H. TAMMEN, MINERALOGIST, 1516 ARAPAHOE ST. DENVER, COLO.

DON'T FORGET ABOUT THE CATALOG.

Solid Vesti
—VIA—

CHICAGO & GRAND TRUNK
AND
GRAND TRUNK RAILWAY

THE MOST DELIGHTFUL

Chicago ... New

VIA THE FAMOUS ST. CLAIR TUNNEL,

Crossing the celebrated Grand Ry. Sus
via the Lehigh Valley Railroad through

Limited Express No. 4, leaving Chicago, Dearborn Station, via
buled Train to New York and Philadelphia. The train runs daily,
Car, first-class Passenger Coaches and Pullman Buffet Sleeping Cars,
BULED, is lighted by gas, heated by steam, and contains all improve
train leaves New York, via LEHIGH VALLEY R. R., 6:00 p.m.; leaves
leaves Niagara Falls, via GRAND TRUNK RY., 7:05 a.m., and arrives

Map showing the Route of the Solid Vestibuled Train between Chicago, New
York and Philadelphia, via CHICAGO & GRAND TRUNK RY., GRAND TRUNK
RY., and the LEHIGH VALLEY RAILROAD, sent for the asking. Address
Passenger Agent nearest to you.

buled Train

AND THE

...PICTURESQUE...

LEHIGH VALLEY Railway

SCENIC ROUTE BETWEEN

York .. Philadelphia

THE WORLD RENOWNED NIAGARA FALLS
pension Bridge in broad daylight, thence
the "SWITZERLAND OF AMERICA."

Chicago & Grand Trunk Ry., at 3:10 p. m., is a Through Solid Vesti-
Sundays included, and consists of a Combination Baggage and Smoking
with Dining Car attached.   THE ENTIRE TRAIN IS VESTI-
ments lately introduced in modern railway equipment.   Returning, this
Philadelphia, via PHILADELPHIA & READING R. R., 6:45 p. m ;
at Chiago, via CHICAGO & GRAND TRUNK RY., at 9 10 p. m.

W. E. DAVIS,	N. J. POWER,	CHAS. S. LEE,
General Passenger Agent.	General Passenger Agent,	General Passenger Agent.
CHIC. & GRAND TRUNK RY.	**GRAND TRUNK RAILWAY,**	**LEHIGH VALLEY RAILROAD,**
CHICAGO ILL.	MONTREAL, CAN.	PHILADELPHIA, PA.

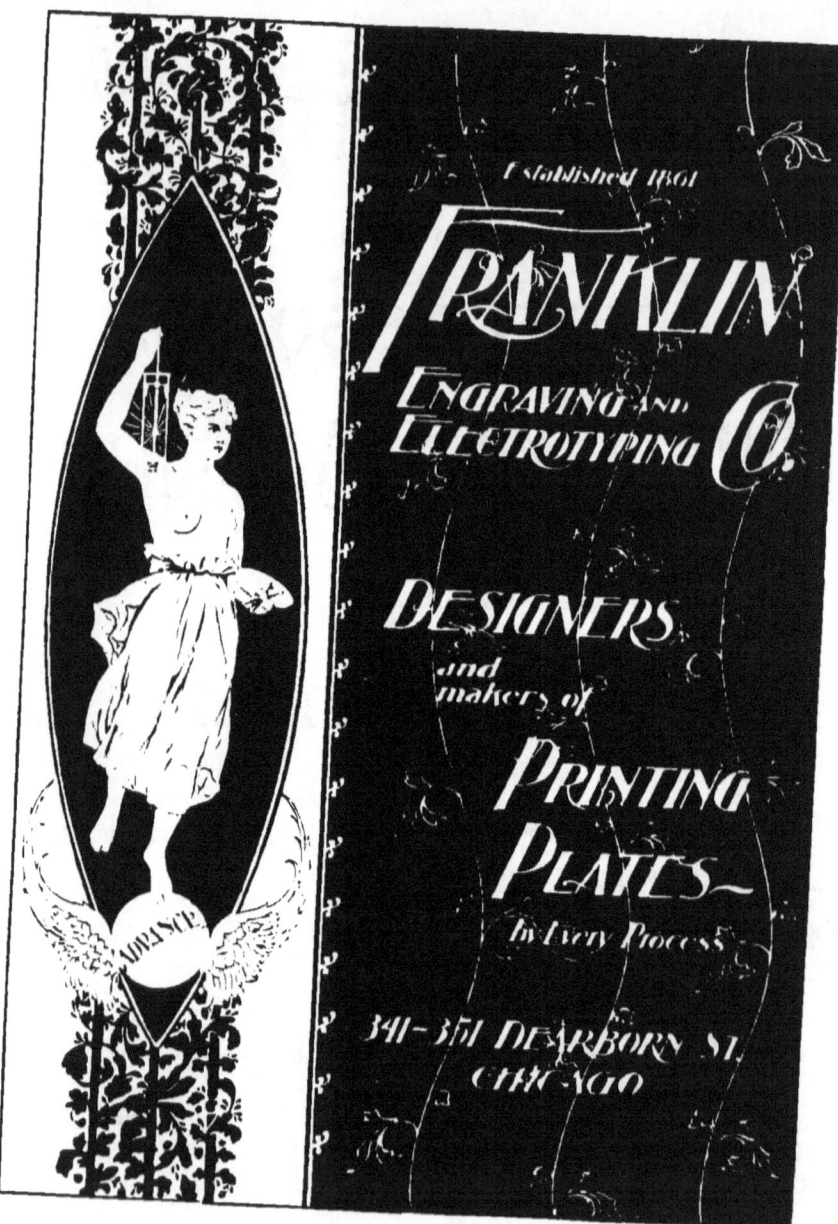

www.ingramcontent.com/pod-product-compliance
Lightning Source LLC
Chambersburg PA
CBHW030316170426
43202CB00009B/1026